Seafood Lover's Almanac

Editor, Mercédès Lee
Contributors: Suzanne Iudicello and Carl Safina

Graphic Design: Amy Herling, MacOmea Design, Glen Cove, New York

Cover art and chapter art by Robert Shetterly (© 1999 National Audubon Society)
Watercolor illustrations © 1999 by Charlotte Knox which first appeared in *Seafood: A Connoisseur's Guide and Cookbook* published by Mitchell Beazley Publishers, and *Seafood Odyssey* published by BBC Worldwide Limited
Computer-generated color illustrations by Richard Upper
Shark and tuna illustrations by © Lisa Osborn which first appeared in *The Forgotten Giants*, a publication of the Ocean Wildlife Campaign and New England Aquarium.

Published in the United States of America by National Audubon Society,
Living Oceans Program

First Edition, October 2000

Printed in Laval, Quebec, by Quebecor Printing, Inc.

ISBN Number 0-9676976-0-3

National Audubon Society and Living Oceans are registered trademarks of the National Audubon Society.

"And all that believed were together,
and all had things common."

Acts of the Apostles

Table of Contents

ACKNOWLEDGMENTS

We give grateful acknowledgment to the following individuals who generously provided their time and expertise to review all or portions of the text: Susan Boa, Beth Clark, Sue Lisin, Daniel Pauly, Doug Rader, Bob Sizemore, Steve Webster, Dave Witting, and several individuals who wish to remain anonymous. While we've made every attempt at accuracy, we take sole responsibility for any errors that may remain. Reviewers should not be held responsible for, or looked upon as endorsing, the judgments contained in this book. All the opinions expressed are those of the authors. We also wish to extend a heart-felt thanks to the following staff of Audubon's Living Oceans program—Sheila Auletti, Merry Camhi, Paul Engelmeyer, Stephanie Glenn, Kerri Kirvin, Bill Krol, and David Wilmot—for reviewing the text, proofreading, fact-checking, image research, and answering public queries. This project could not have been done without their professional efforts, sense of humor, and unwavering moral support. There were also many others in the trenches of conservation, research, fishing, seafood processing, and management who shared their knowledge with us along the way for which we are eternally grateful. In addition, Lidia Mattichio Bastianich, Robin Downey, Jerry Speir and Barbara Ewell, the Lesh family, the Moosewood Collective, Nora Pouillon, Pat Tummons, and David Waltuck contributed tasty recipes, sharing their joy of cooking and seafood. Portions of the salmon profile were taken and adapted with permission from *Song for the Blue Ocean: Encounters Along the World's Coasts and Beneath the Seas* (first edition, 1998, New York, Henry Holt) by Carl Safina. This project was made possible through the generous support of the David and Lucile Packard Foundation, the Oak Foundation, the Norcross Wildlife Foundation, the Curtis and Edith Munson Foundation, the Pew Charitable Trusts, Royal Caribbean International, the French Foundation, and the Wallace Research Foundation.

This National Audubon Society Living Oceans book is available for special promotions and premiums. For details, contact: Audubon's Living Oceans Program, 550 South Bay Ave., Islip, NY 11751

Seafood Lover's Almanac

NATIONAL AUDUBON SOCIETY

Mercédès Lee, Editor

Contributors: Suzanne Iudicello and Carl Safina

Introduction

This book is, above all, a celebration of fish.

As any seafood connoisseur knows from the perspective of palate, not all fish are equal. Their many differences also extend to their living styles, where they come from, how they're caught, how fishing is managed, and how they're doing. Though the ready availability of seafood in the marketplace can lead to the false impression that all is well, some fish are doing distinctly better than others. *Seafood Lover's Almanac* explores these elements and, I hope, can help you become more familiar with the seafood you eat. This book's illustrative and whimsical art allows a pictorial exploration of fact and fantasy surrounding fish and our health-conscious preoccupations. *In the Wild* delves into the natural and sometimes eccentric lives of all the species profiled. Nutrition and health information, alternative choices to depleted species, and the forms they're found in the marketplace, are interspersed throughout. And to help navigate through the confusing labyrinth of nomenclature, we've included proper scientific names, common names, regional nicknames, and marketplace pseudonyms. Lastly, but certainly not least, we rank species from GREEN to YELLOW to RED on our signature icon, the Audubon Fish Scale.

Our goal is to help you become more familiar with the seafood you buy, enabling you to make choices toward more abundant, better-managed species. We are not organizing a boycott on any species, fishing outfit, operation, processor, or company, and the information contained here should not be construed as such. We believe that the best consumer is an informed one.

Almost everything we do affects nature and carries an "ecological footprint." Revealing the environmental costs associated with everyday products and giving people the opportunity to make better, more informed choices is fast becoming the standard. Learning in the 1980s that recycling is good for the environment, people separated paper, cans, and plastic in their households for curb-side pickup. Recycling created a whole new industry in our economy. A recent nutritional supplement labeling debate in Congress elicited more than a million letters from the public asking for health-friendly and better product disclosure regulations. This massive outpouring of public opinion was the greatest ever received on any issue on Capitol Hill. These examples of singular personal actions speak in no small way to the collective strength of consumer choice.

Consumer advocacy is now extending to food from the oceans, which makes sense because marine creatures are the only wild animals still hunted commercially on a large scale, and consumer demand drives fishing. The power of consumers to influence the buying decisions of seafood wholesalers and retailers has rarely been tried, but its effects have in some cases been dramatic. Consumer reaction to dolphin deaths in the major Pacific tuna fishery led to "dolphin safe" labeling, complete restructuring of the tuna fishery, and a huge reduction in dolphin deaths. A more recent "Give Swordfish a Break" campaign—run by SeaWeb and the Natural Resources Defense Council—raised visibility, affected prices, and gathered crucial momentum towards a recovery plan for depleted swordfish in the Atlantic.

Projects initiated by environmental organizations, businesses, and private-sector partnerships are beginning to emerge specifically aimed at using the power of consumer choice in the marketplace to prompt more effective management and improved conservation. Some restaurants and aquariums have begun to take steps on their own to tackle the difficult question of what seafood is ecologically best to serve. The Monterey Bay Aquarium in California and the John G. Shedd Aquarium in Chicago, for example, have in-house restaurants and catering services whose menus are determined by thoughtful seafood-buying practices. And they adapt their menus depending on changes in species' status and other new information. In the larger marketplace, consumers may soon be able to select fish products certified by the nonprofit Marine Stewardship Council as sustainably caught, and marked with an on-pack logo. Another, the Cape Cod Commercial Hook Fishermen's Association is working with local fishermen and businesses in New England to promote hook-caught fish as an alternative to fish caught with habitat-destroying trawl nets. The first of its kind, Ecofish.com is an internet-based sustainable seafood retail business. Their mission is to provide ecologically responsible seafood from healthy and properly managed marine fisheries and to use some of their profits to support conservation.

Some seafoods carry less environmental impact than others because of differences in their abundance, how they're caught, and how well fishing is managed. The key is to know which species are in good shape, which are not, and why. This is where the Audubon Fish Scale can help.

We created the Fish Scale to make it easy for people to see at a glance how a particular species is doing. Our ranking system is somewhat subjective—it's only our opinion—but it's based on careful assessment of the following criteria:

• Life history: Does it take years to start breeding? Does it have few or many offspring? Do they live a long or short natural lifespan? Does it have special vulnerabilities like nest-guarding or spawning in large groups that make the fish particularly easy targets for fishing?

• Management record: Is it overfished? Are measures in place to rebuild depleted species? Are managers correcting problems like habitat-destroying gear?

• Habitat health: Is the species' habitat intact enough to sustain healthy populations or rebuild depleted species? (Sometimes coastal development and pollution problems inhibit the natural ability of fishes to rebound even if fishing pressure is relaxed.) Is habitat destroyed in the process of fishing for this species?

• By-kill: Are other creatures caught in the process of targeting this species or is this species incidentally caught in the fishing gear targeting other species? Is the level of bycatch significant and problematic?

Abundant, well-managed, low-bycatch species rate a GREEN on our Fish Scale. If there are some concerns about a species' status, fishing methods, or management, it ranks in the YELLOW. Species with significant problems receive a RED designation on our Fish Scale.

Many fishers and managers are doing their best for the long-term future of their fishery. Some fish were difficult for us to rate because depletions are the result of past management or natural factors. For instance, suppose a fish is severely depleted from past overfishing, but a new recovery plan will let the fish rebuild. Reasonable people can disagree over whether such a fish should be avoided until it begins rebuilding, or whether the recovery plan is an adequate reason to recommend to consumers that the fishery has now become a sustainable enterprise. (We would be inclined to rate it YELLOW.) Or, consider a species like Atlantic salmon, endangered in the wild and widely farmed. Most farms cause problems for wild salmon runs, but Maine salmon farms use significantly better practices than many others. (We rate farmed salmon RED overall, but point out the difference with Maine farmed salmon so consumers can look for it or ask their market to carry it.)

Making full use of the *Seafood Lover's Almanac* depends on you knowing what species you're choosing and where it comes from. Seafood origins (and even accurate names) are many times unavailable to consumers. For example, Georges Bank Atlantic cod are rebuilding under effective management and we would rate them YELLOW, while other sub-populations in the region are doing very poorly and remain in the RED. But there's currently no way for a consumer to know which in the market are cod from Georges Bank. In cases like this, we try to suggest alternative fish unless you're confident of the source. The only way around this problem is to ask questions. The more consumers ask, the more seafood sellers will recognize the need to provide better information.

There are certain species for which accurate name and origin information are effectively used as a sales tool to attract consumers. For example, take Alaska wild salmon, dungeness crab, and shellfish. Whole marketing and tracking systems exist to follow the trail of these "boutique species" from point of catch to point of sale. If it works for boutique species, it can work for all species. So, for your discerning palate and the sake of food from the sea, *Just Ask*—What species is it? and Where does it come from? It may take time, but the market will follow to make this information more readily and universally available.

Meanwhile, enjoy, knowing your choices can help heal the seas.

Mercédès Lee
Islip, New York
March 2000

King Cod & the Royal Court

Cod • Haddock, Monkfish, Tilefish • Lingcod & Black Cod • Pollock

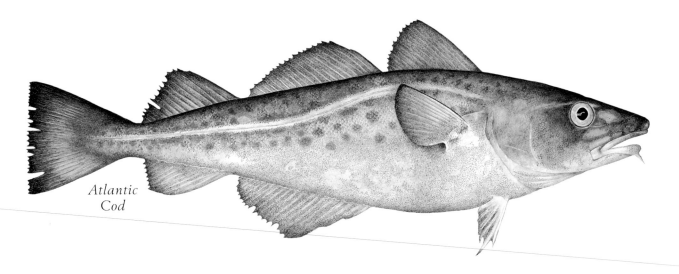

Atlantic
Cod

Atlantic & Pacific Cod

Fish
Scale

Pacific Cod

In the Wild: Only minor details in appearance distinguish the closely related Atlantic and Pacific cods. Atlantic cod come in a variety of hues: brown, reddish brown, orange, brick-red, black, gray, green. Its Pacific cousin is a little more subdued, in brown to gray with a light belly and dusky, white-tipped fins. Both have that cute little fleshy goatee or "barbel" on the chin that says "I'm a cod!" Scientists believe this appendage helps them feel the ocean floor. Cod grow fast and die young. Females lay more than a million eggs at each spawning which then drift with the winds and currents. Juvenile cod reside in upper-level waters feeding on barnacle larvae and such until they grow to a size where they "drop" to the bottom. Their diets change to eating just about anything, but unlike most classic bottom-feeders, cod will sometimes chase fish to the surface if they're so inclined. Its dominantly white flesh indicates a body built of muscle designed for short bursts.

Atlantic cod occur from western Greenland south to Cape Hatteras, North Carolina. The eastern Atlantic from Russia and the Baltic to the Bay of Biscay also harbor Atlantic cod, these being of a separate breeding population from that off the U.S. Speaking of breeding, many of our Atlantic cod spawn in winter in the Gulf of Maine. There are also separate breeding populations in the Grand Banks and Georges Bank areas. In better times, the Atlantic species typically grew to 50 or even 100 pounds. A 211 pounder of more than six-feet long was report-

OVERALL RECOMMENDATION:

RED on the Fish Scale if from the Atlantic; GREEN if from the Pacific. If you're not inclined to question your waiter or grocer about where their fish came from, skip the cod. But, if you're willing to ask questions and read labels, you can still enjoy this most popular of fish. Ask for Pacific cod or hook-caught Atlantic cod. Alaska pollock is also a good choice in place of cod.

Cod: fresh; whole; steaks; fillets; frozen fillets and blocks; salt cod

Atlantic
Cod

edly caught in 1895 on a longline off the Massachusetts coast. Sadly, they now average less than ten pounds—fishing pressure keeps their lives short.

Pacific cod extend from the Bering Sea to Oregon, and occasionally as far south as northern California. These cod spawn in wintertime in the Gulf of Alaska, and move inshore and offshore as the seasons change, preferring cooler waters. They swim at the surface down to 1,500 feet deep. Some Pacific cod grow longer than three feet, but not commonly.

How They're Doing: As one of the world's most important commercial fishes, there's been much ado about Atlantic cod since the 1500s. Indeed, with ships and salt and will, Europeans came to North American waters in search of the reported multitudes of fish to catch and cure and bring home. Soon after, cod became cause for French and British settlement of North America. The fishery was sustainable for nearly five centuries. But our capacity to catch fish following post World War II industrialization of America's fishing fleets quickly outstripped the biological capacity of the fish. After several decades of modern industrial overfishing and mismanagement in the Atlantic, they're—not surprisingly—doing extremely poorly. So bad, in fact, they've been designated commercially extinct in certain areas. "The problem," says Mark Kurlansky in his exceptional book, *Cod: A Biography of the Fish That Changed the World*, "...is that they [current fishers] are at the wrong end of a 1,000-year fishing spree." In the Gulf of Maine in particular, cod are so depleted, biologists fear the possibility of collapse. On New England's Georges Bank and areas to the south, surveys show continuing declines from an already low level. Cod are overfished in other areas of the North Atlantic as well, including the "Icelandic cod" you might see in markets. In the Pacific and off Alaska, however, cod are still abundant.

NUTRITION: COD

90 calories
0 fat calories
total fat 0.5 g
45 mg cholesterol
20 g protein

(Based on a 3 oz. serving size. Vitamins and minerals are based on 2,000 calorie diet.)

Pacific Cod

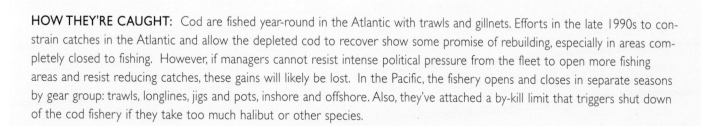

HOW THEY'RE CAUGHT: Cod are fished year-round in the Atlantic with trawls and gillnets. Efforts in the late 1990s to constrain catches in the Atlantic and allow the depleted cod to recover show some promise of rebuilding, especially in areas completely closed to fishing. However, if managers cannot resist intense political pressure from the fleet to open more fishing areas and resist reducing catches, these gains will likely be lost. In the Pacific, the fishery opens and closes in separate seasons by gear group: trawls, longlines, jigs and pots, inshore and offshore. Also, they've attached a by-kill limit that triggers shut down of the cod fishery if they take too much halibut or other species.

Atlantic Cod

(G. morhua)

Pacific Cod

(G. macrocephalus)

On Eating Them: "Scrod" can mean cod or haddock. In the old days when there was a greater difference between big fish and small fish caught, "scrod" was a general term referring to the small size market category of either cod or haddock. There also used to be two spellings. If it was spelled "SCROD" it was a small cod. If it was "SCHROD" it was a small haddock.

Special Issues: Because the primary gear for catching cod is the otter trawl, by-kill is high, including young cod that are critical for rebuilding. Bottom trawl gear used also destroys or degrades habitat for this and a host of other species. The Cape Cod Commercial Hook Fishermen's Association is working with local fishermen and businesses in Cape Cod and the surrounding area to promote hook-caught fish, a very good alternative to fish caught with habitat-destroying nets.

Markets: Primary consumers of cod are Japan, Korea, Norway, Great Britain, Germany, Canada, and Southeast Asia. The main exporting countries are Canada, Iceland, Norway, Russia, and the U.S.

Trawl Gear: Large bag-shaped nets, open at one end, towed by a boat to catch fish between the surface and the bottom.

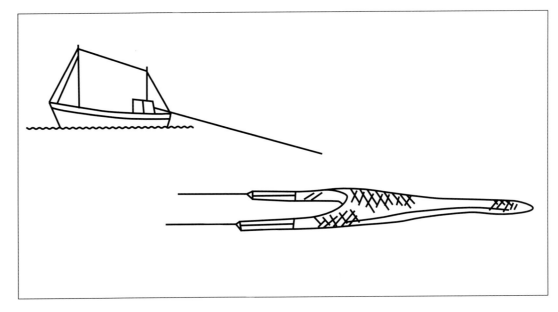

Haddock

Haddock, Monkfish & Tilefish

OVERALL RECOMMENDATION:

These are YELLOW to RED on the Fish Scale because they're over-fished, depleted, and they suffer habitat problems because of the methods used to catch them. Stick with the striped bass or tilapia as substitutes.

Fish Scale

In the Wild: There are about three dozen species of "groundfish" found off the North American coast from the Canadian maritimes to North Carolina. Although they bear the collective name "groundfish" because they stay close to the bottom and are usually found together, these species are as different from each other as carrots from cabbages. Groundfish run the gamut of fishy sizes, shapes, colors and behavior. They vary from the the iridescent and rainbow-hued tilefish to the grotesque brown monkfish with its chin flaps and dangling protuberances, to the streamlined haddock. Haddock can run to about two feet; tilefish and monkfish can grow four feet or longer. Monkfish are significant carnivores, and sport an array of long, sharp teeth. The monkfish has been described as one big mouth with a tail.

Groundfish occur from estuaries to the nearshore shelf to deep channels and holes. As they move about the bottom, some in schools (haddock), others as loners (tilefish, monkfish), these species consume a variety of worms, small crustaceans, clams, shellfishes, squid, and small fish, all collected from the ocean bottom or near-so.

Tilefish has a very distinguished appearance, graced with a prominent fleshy fin-like flap on its forehead, and blushy-tints of red on both sides of its face and yellow spots on its body. So large a fish (growing more than 50 pounds) remained surprisingly elusive in the Northeast until 1879 when a certain Captain Kirby caught one while cod fishing in 150 fathoms of water south of Nantucket Shoals Lightship. Shortly after, the federal government identified

Monkfish

Tilefish

Haddock

Haddock: fillets
Monkfish: cheeks, liver, and tail only used and sold as fillets
Tilefish: fillets

Tilefish

**NUTRITION:
HADDOCK**

100 calories
10 fat calories
1 g total fat
80 mg cholesterol
21 g protein
6% iron

(Based on a 3 oz. serving size. Vitamins and minerals are based on 2,000 calorie diet.)

Haddock
(M. aeglefinus)

Monkfish *(West Atlantic: L. americanus; East Atlantic: L. piscaotrius; Indo-Pacific: L. Litulon)*: goosefish, bellyfish, allmouth, lawyer, anglerfish

Tilefish *(L. chamaeleonticeps)*: golden snapper, tile bass, white snapper

it as a resource aplenty worthy of targeting for commerce and American tables. But within three years of its discovery, more than a billion tilefish were found floating dead on the ocean surface, from Delaware Bay north. An unusual intrusion of warm water into normally cold water was believed to have caused this disaster, as other species suffered as well. Gone but not extinct, the fish reappeared in 1887, and again won a place at American tables, more or less. This, with a little help from the government which again undertook a marketing initiative to popularize the fish to varying degrees of success. Tilefish are burrowers in submarine canyon walls and are very dependent on this habitat for shelter. Tilefish, studies later affirmed, are cursed with having to live in a very limited temperature range. It makes one wonder what global climate change will mean for this ocean aristocrat.

The **monkfish**, with a number of relatives in the abyssal Atlantic, looks like a deep-sea monster. Indeed, it is one fish you will never mistake for another if you ever happen to see it in its entirety. Known since ancient times as the "fishing frog" (not to be confused with one anglerfish called "frogfish") maybe because of its big lippy mouth and protruding filament atop its head to lure prey. It appears to be quite the predator, with a remarkable appetite for feasting on eels, dogfish, alewives, menhaden, tautog, seabass, puffers, cod, flounder, haddock, lobsters, crabs, and seabirds, among many other sea ceatures. All, of course, depending on what's available. It's amazing to think that monkfish actually catch seabirds, as the fish is a dedicated bottom-

HOW THEY'RE CAUGHT: Historically, many of these groundfish species were bycatch in the once abundant and lucrative cod fisheries of New England. Proving once again that one man's trash is another's treasure, these fish that previously had no market have become the target of the groundfish fleet now that cod is so scarce. Commercial fishers use trawls, gillnets, longlines to catch these and other groundfish from the Grand Banks southward to the Outer Banks of North Carolina.

dweller, but historical accounts (one record places seven ducks in a monkfish stomach!) and recent autopsy records are clear about this. A remarkable feature distinguishing this family of anglerfishes, to which the monkfish is a full-fledged member, is the fishing lure. This protuberance is very light with a fleshy lure at the end and can be angled and tapped in any direction to attract potential prey. This fish camouflages well, lying flat as it does on the bottom. It opens its mouth with such a surprising sucking force that in one blink its unsuspecting visitor-turned-food is gone, devoured. Its expandable belly allows the monkfish to engulf very large prey longer than itself!

How They're Doing: Like cod and flounder, many of these lesser known groundfish have also suffered from what was probably the world's greatest fishery management disaster. Several decades of mismanagement and overfishing left them depleted, at terrible social cost in New England and the Canadian maritimes. Although severely depleted, haddock may be showing some signs of recovery under severe fishing restrictions, benefitting, in fact, from entirely closed areas in both the Gulf of Maine and Georges Bank. Tilefish and monkfish are overfished. For decades they were accounted for only as bycatch in the directed fisheries for cod, haddock and flounder, but received increased management attention in the late 1990s when the fleets began targeting them in the absence of formerly preferred species. As a result of stepped-up management, they may have a chance for recovery.

Special Issues: All these species are victims of direct overfishing, by-kill, and habitat degradation. By-kill in trawling is second only to the notoriously poor shrimp fisheries. Bottom trawling causes significant bycatch. It also destroys or degrades habitat by raking the ocean bottom. This cripples affected ecosystems by lowering the productivity and recovery potential of vast areas.

Markets: The haddock offered for sale in the U.S. comes mostly from Norway, Iceland, and the United Kingdom, since the U.S. supply is nearly non-existent. But if you're tempted to eat "Icelandic haddock," remember this: haddock are overfished nearly everywhere.

Monkfish

Lingcod

Lingcod & Black Cod

Fish
Scale

Alaska
Lingcod
Black Cod

Other
Lingcod

In the Wild: Neither sablefish (black cod) nor lingcod are actually cods. Common near the coast, **lingcod** range from Baja California to Kodiak Island, Alaska. Lingcod off Alaska breed separately from those off Washington and south. Lingcod grow big, reaching five feet long. They live on the bottom pretty much as loners and don't migrate except that the offshore individuals will move inshore to spawn in winter. Males establish territories before spawning and guard the fertilized eggs until they hatch (about 6-7 weeks), frequently fanning them to keep them oxygenated. This dedication presumably prevents predators from feeding on their successors. When nest-guarding, lingcod are vulnerable to spearfishing because they will not abandon their incubating eggs even when a diver comes near.

OVERALL
RECOMMENDATION:

Alaskan lingcod and black cod (most commonly known as sablefish) are relatively abundant and offer an alternative to depleted Atlantic cod. They rate a GREEN on the Fish Scale. However, lingcod off California, Washington, Oregon, and British Columbia are overfished, and we consider them in the YELLOW zone of the Fish Scale. Even though a rebuilding plan is in place, certain traits leave them vulnerable. If you want the lingcod, ask if it comes from Alaska.

Sleek and dark green to black, **sablefish** school among their own and live in a range of depths from surface inshore waters down to more than 9,000 feet. Sablefish mature young but live long—more than 60 years. The older the fish, the deeper it'll be. They occur in the North Pacific off Japan, in the Bering Sea where they spawn, and south to the Baja California Peninsula. They eat squid, various invertebrates and numerous species of fish. Halibut, lingcod, and sea lions, to name a few, feast on them. Killer whales and even sperm whales sometimes take sablefish from longline gear as it is being hauled back into the ship.

Lingcod: fresh; frozen
Sablefish: fresh; smoked; and also is sometimes used in surimi

How They're Doing: Lingcod are depleted and overfished south of Alaska but managers have put measures in place to help them recover. There's not much, if any, mixing of these with the lingcod off Alaska which are in much better shape. Sablefish, while apparently still at healthy levels, have been declining since the late 1980s because of changing oceanic conditions, their popularity in seafood dishes, and the consumer demand that drives fishing for them.

How They're Caught: Lingcod has been called the "heart and soul" of bottomfishing along the California coast. Indeed, they're a favorite of recreational fishers on party boats and private boats because they get big and are good fighters, not to mention good eating. Spearfishers also hunt them, revelling in the chase and fight. In fact, it's not uncommon for towns and tackle shops to hold lingcod tournaments offering monetary prizes for the best catch. Commercially, fishers use gillnets and trawls to catch lingcod all along the Pacific. Similarly, commercial fishers use trawls, traps, or longlines to catch sablefish.

fish names

Lingcod
(O. elongatus): Ling

Black Cod
(A. fimbria): Sablefish

Black Cod

Is eating fish is good for your heart? YES.

For many years, nutritionists wondered why Eskimos, who eat foods containing lots of polyunsaturated fats, didn't develop heart disease. Researchers found the link between the absence of heart disease and the oil in the fish they and other northern people ate as a principal part of their diet. Fish oil contains what are called "Omega-3s." These are polyunsaturated fatty acids found almost exclusively in fish and shellfish. Medical researchers found that men who ate fish two or three times a week lived longer than those who did not, and they had less heart disease.

Omega–3s are believed to reduce blood clotting, relax the arteries, and change the chemistry that affects heartbeat, blood flow and other blood vessel actions. These fatty acids have little affect on blood cholesterol levels, but they do lower blood fats and blood pressure, and discourage the build-up of arterial "plaque." Beneficial Omega-3s are found almost exclusively in fish, particularly richer species like mackerel, salmon, tuna, and sardines.

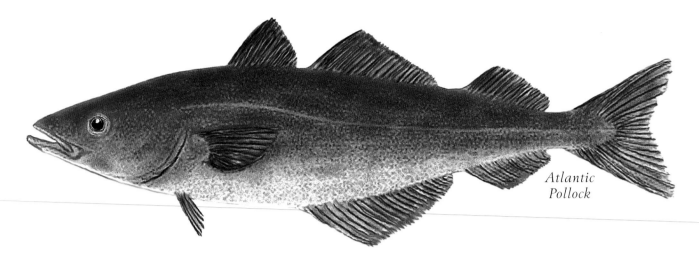

Atlantic Pollock

Pollock

Pacific Pollock

In the Wild: A member of the cod family, **Pacific pollock**—particularly off Alaska—is the world's most abundant food fish. A small two-pound, streamlined fish, pollock are olive green to brown with a silvery underside and large eyes. They inhabit waters from the central California coast north to the Bering Sea, and west to Russia and the Sea of Japan. It's presumed there are three separate breeding populations. Pollock move in large schools and feed on species such as capelin and herring. Pollock, particularly the juveniles, are important food for seabirds and marine mammals.

Atlantic pollock, also greenish brown with a silver-gray belly, is a much larger fish than its Pacific counterpart, sometimes growing to 25 pounds, though market size is between four and 10 pounds. They mature by six years old. Pollock is found on both sides of the North Atlantic, and has dozens of local names in the U.K. In the northwest Atlantic they can be found on the western Scotian shelf and in the Gulf of Maine, and they move between the shelf and Georges Bank.

How They're Doing: Alaska pollock are abundant, although in the late 1990s there were signs that they were beginning to decline. Ecosystem studies are underway to try to determine the nature of this change, which is crucial to do given the critical stature of these pollock as an important food source for humans and other creatures.

OVERALL
RECOMMENDATION:

Pacific pollock is GREEN on the Audubon Fish Scale. Though used primarily in seafood products, pollock itself is an excellent substitute for any mild, white fish, such as cod. Atlantic pollock falls in the RED zone on the Fish Scale because it's depleted from many years of overfishing and hasn't yet been restored to abundance.

fish names

Pacific Pollock
(*T. chalcogramma*): walleye pollock, bigeye cod, Pacific Tomcod

Atlantic Pollock
(*P. virens*): European pollock, pollack, blue cod

Atlantic Pollock

Alaska pollock: boneless fillets; breaded nuggets; surimi (a fish paste used as a food additive and to manufacture imitation seafood); pollock roe for Japanese dishes

There are many fewer Atlantic pollock than there were historically because for a long time they were overfished and natural conditions kept them from successfully bringing new generations into the population. While there are signs that they're doing better, they have far to go.

In the 1800s, Atlantic pollock were scorned by fishermen who believed these fish preyed on valuable species such as cod and haddock. Nonetheless, some fishers using seines did target Atlantic pollock for their liver oil. Subsequently, pollock became by-kill in the trawl nets of groundfishers, and it's been only since the 1980s that fishers began directly targeting pollock off New England and Canada.

How They're Caught:
Off Alaska, fishers catch Pacific pollock using mid-water trawls. Pollock are caught and delivered to onshore processors, as well as caught and processed at sea. Some pollock are also taken incidentally by pot and longline fishers targetting other species. The North Pacific pollock fishery is often pointed to as an exemplary management regime, but is not without its problems (see "Special Issues" below). Managers set conservation-minded catch limits; require that observers be on board fishing boats targeting Pacific pollock to monitor what's going on; and apply creative techniques to reduce by-kill.

Special Issues:
There are concerns about the connection between pollock catches and declines of Stellers sea lions and some seabirds that rely on young Pacific pollock for food. Several interesting techniques have been employed to reduce by-kill in the Pacific pollock fishery, most notably peer-pressure brought about by publication of the names of the vessels and skippers who exceed their by-kill limits.

NUTRITION: POLLOCK

90 calories
10 fat calories
total fat 1.0 g
80 mg cholesterol
20 g protein

(Based on a 3 oz. serving size. Vitamins and minerals are based on 2,000 calorie diet.)

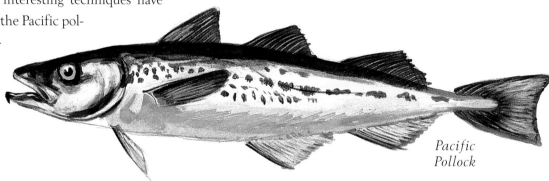

Pacific Pollock

ON EATING THEM: Atlantic pollock is darker, oilier, and stronger tasting than its Pacific counterpart. Pacific pollock is the principal fish used for fish sticks, prepared frozen fish products such as seasoned, grilled fish fillets, battered fillets, and the ubiquitous school lunch and fast food fish sandwiches. For example, the fish in Gorton's fish fillets (breaded, battered, grilled/seasoned) is Alaska pollock. The fish in the McDonald's fish sandwich is also Alaska pollock.

"It is probably impossible for any-
one now alive to comprehend the
magnitude of fish life in the waters
of the New World when the
European invasion began...
According to the records [early
voyagers] have left us, they seem
to have been overwhelmed by the
glut of fishes."

– *Farley Mowat,* Sea of Slaughter

The Flatlanders
Plaice, Sole, Flounder • Halibut

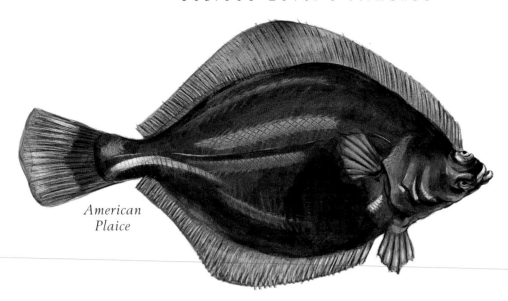

*American
Plaice*

Plaice, Sole & Flounder

In the Wild: Flounder, plaice, and sole are among the "flatfishes," so-called because they're...well...flat. They have both eyes on one side of the body, with their white flat side always facing the ocean bottom. But they don't start out that way. As larvae, they're pretty ordinary, looking like baby fish too small for their big eyes, swimming upright. Then, in a true metamorphical wonder, one eye migrates to pair up with the other, and from then on the fish lives sideways, as a righty or lefty, on the ocean floor (see illustration, p. 24). Scientists think that eye migration is genetically triggered, but water temperature has a lot to do with how long the transformation takes. In general, eye migration among the flatfishes can take as little as one day and as long as 60 days. In a winter flounder, eye migration starts after the larva is 20 days old and takes a mere one to two days from start to finish. For one eye to move to the other side of the head requires a great deal of energy and considerable rearrangement of bones, blood vessels, muscles, nerves, and the like.

Flounders and their kin appear to be honest, elegant, and dainty fishes, almost vulnerable, but they're really true artists at deception and ambush. They patiently lie on a patch of sandy ocean floor and without a thought become nearly invisible, adjusting the coloration and patterns on their exposed body to match that of the sea floor. With absolute surprising agility and speed they flick their tail and in an instant devour unsuspecting prey passing by. When they swim they remain horizontal to the ocean floor, adjusting their bodies to move in wave-like fashion. American plaice, by the way, can live 26 years, maturing when they're about six years old. The other smaller flounders live much shorter lives.

**OVERALL
RECOMMENDATION:**

RED on the Fish Scale for these flatfish if from the Atlantic because they're overfished and depleted; GREEN if from the Pacific because they're abundant, except Dover sole, and well-managed .

Flounder, Plaice, Sole: whole; fresh or frozen; fillets; stuffed; and breaded
Rex Sole: sometimes ground into fertilizer

The Flatlanders

NUTRITION: FLOUNDER AND SOLE

100 calories
14 fat calories
total fat 1.5 g
60 mg cholesterol
21 g protein

(Based on a 3 oz. serving size. Vitamins and minerals are based on 2,000 calorie diet.)

By the time they're flat, they've become benthic (bottom-dwelling) creatures, where they eat worms, crustaceans, and generally small things that pass by. Each species has its preferred depth of habitation, from lagoons, bays, shallow estuaries, to the deep sea. Yellowtail flounder, for example, typically live in waters around 50 feet deep. Dover sole prefer muddy bottoms to 4,800 feet deep. When they're grown-up fish (not larvae), flatfish migrate mostly onshore-offshore as opposed to up and down the coast. For example, summer flounder prefer estuaries in summer and deep offshore continental shelf areas come winter.

How They're Doing: As their variety and range suggests, these fishes are proud catches for recreational and commercial fishers alike, and good eating, too. The Pacific flatfishes are abundant and none is classified as overfished. The story on the Atlantic side, though, is less rosy. American plaice, summer flounder, winter flounder, witch flounder, and windowpane flounder are all depleted and overfished. Yellowtail flounder is at an extremely low population level, but beginning to show signs of recovering. Regardless, all of the Atlantic flounders, even the ones showing some signs of rebuilding, are critically depleted.

In New England, the story of flounders is the same as that of other notoriously over-exploited groundfish. Only with severe restrictions will there be a chance for these fish to recover. But it's not easy, and there's constant pressure from fishers responding to consumer demand to continue overfishing.

Yellowtail Flounder

How They're Caught: Commercial fishers catch flatfish principally by trawl gear, but also with longlines. In the Pacific, conservation measures include limiting catches, permits, size limits, and seasonal and area restrictions. In Alaska, because bycatch of halibut in other flatfish fisheries is strictly managed, the fishery usually is shut down for the sake of halibut well before catch limits of the other flatfish are reached.

fish names

American Plaice *(H. platessoides)*: dab

Dover Sole *(M. pacificus)* Not to be confused with the E. Atlantic fish that Europeans also call dover sole *(S. solea)*

English Sole *(P. vetula)*

Petrale Sole *(E. jordani)*: brill

Rex Sole *(G. zachirus)*: longfinned sole, witch (not to be confused with the witch flounder in the Atlantic, *(G. cynoglossus)*

Summer Flounder *(P. dentatus)*: fluke

Windowpane *(S. aquosus)*: sundial

Winter Flounder *(P. americanus)*: lemon sole, also called dab in Canada, black back flounder

Witch Flounder *(G. cynoglossus)*

Yellowfin Sole *(L. aspera)*

Yellowtail Flounder *(P. ferrugineus)*

…and many others

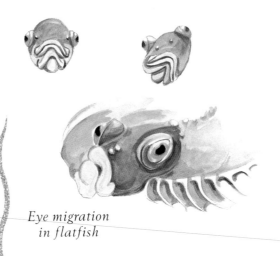

Eye migration in flatfish

"HANDEDNESS" IN FLATFISH

Flatfish are identified by their "handedness." Many have attempted to explain which way is right-handed or left-handed in these flatfish, but the ensuing conversation inevitably ends up in an Abbot and Costello-like comedy skit. Here's our attempt to explain:

1. Place the fish flat as it would normally lay in the wild, white side down, eyes and dark side up;

2. Arrange the fish so that its pectoral fin is below the lateral line (indicating that its stomach contents are on the lower half);

3. See what direction the mouth is pointing: a left-handed individual will have its mouth pointing left; a right-handed fish will have its mouth pointing to the right.

This might seem an esoteric exercise, deciphering righties from lefties, but it's a key ingredient to differentiate between similar-looking fish.

In the case of summer flounder, some years more fish are caught recreationally than commercially. Unfortunately, this is one example where commercial fishers and recreational fishers find themselves bitter enemies fighting over a diminishing living resource, with the fish caught in the middle. The story of wise King Solomon comes to mind, when two mothers claim to have given birth to the same baby and they need him to resolve this dispute over ownership. Solomon suggests the baby be cut in half. In doing so he focuses concern on the welfare of the baby and away from the bickering parties. Perhaps there's a lesson there.

Special Issues: Since most flatfish are caught by trawls, by-kill of other species is a considerable problem. Inadvertent catch and discard of juveniles is a particular concern in the summer flounder fishery. Catching juvenile American plaice in shrimp trawls was once a serious problem, but a technological innovation called a "fish excluder" device reduced that problem substantially. Bottom trawling is also very hard on habitat.

WHERE THEY LIVE:

American Plaice:	Atlantic Ocean from Grand Banks to Rhode Island
Dover Sole:	Pacific Ocean, principally off California, but occurring from Baja California to Alaska
English Sole:	Pacific Ocean, principally off California, but occurring from Baja California to Alaska
Petrale Sole:	Pacific Ocean, principally off California, but occurring from Baja California to Alaska
Rex Sole:	Pacific Ocean, principally off California, but occurring from Baja California to Alaska
Summer Flounder:	Atlantic Ocean from Gulf of Maine to South Carolina
Windowpane:	Atlantic Ocean from Gulf of St. Lawrence to northern Florida
Winter Flounder:	Atlantic Ocean from Labrador to Georgia, mostly concentrated between Gulf of St. Lawrence and Chesapeake Bay
Witch Flounder:	Atlantic Ocean from Gulf of St. Lawrence and Grand Banks to North Carolina Also in the East Atlantic.
Yellowfin Sole, Arrowtooth Flounder:	Pacific Ocean off Alaska
Yellowtail Flounder:	Atlantic Ocean from Gulf of St. Lawrence to Chesapeake Bay

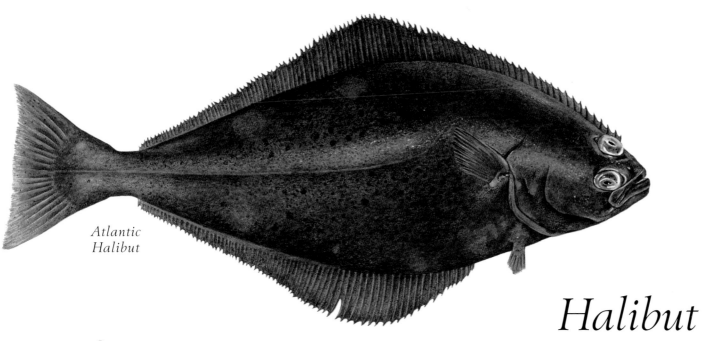

Atlantic Halibut

Halibut

Fish Scale

Pacific Halibut →

California Halibut

OVERALL RECOMMENDATION:

Take caution to know from whence your halibut hails. On the Fish Scale it falls in the RED if from the Atlantic. Pacific and California halibut rank GREEN because they're abundant and well managed. The size, texture, and taste of Pacific halibut steaks make them suitable substitutes for swordfish, especially for grilling.

In the Wild: Mostly, halibuts are known for their size (and of course their delicate taste). They're the largest of the flounder-like flatfish, and veritable behemoths they be. Historically, **Atlantic halibut** lived as many as 40 years, matured when they were about eight years old, and weighed as much as 700 pounds. Now, they more typically reach around 100 pounds. Male **Pacific halibut** typically push the scales to 200 pounds, but they can reach eight feet, 500 pounds. One was seen completely draped over and covering the hood of a Toyota Land Cruiser—a fish of questionable quality after that mode of transport! No slouch in the size category, **California halibut** can grow five feet long, but only tip in at 72 pounds maximum.

All three species are olive-brown to black on the "eyed" side, and whitish underneath, but for variety, the California halibut is sometimes tinged with a lighter-shade of green or orange. Pacific and Atlantic halibut are right-handed fish, but to confuse matters, California halibut can have eyes on its right or left as its genes see fit. (See "Handedness in Flatfish" on page 24.)

The Atlantic species ranges from New Jersey to Greenland, along the European coast south to the English Channel. Pacific halibut occur in an oceanic arc from the Sea of Japan to the Bering Sea and south to Baja California, but are rarely seen south of Oregon. The Atlantic and Pacific halibuts are deepwater fish, preferring soft bottoms from 200 to as deep as 3,000 feet. Juveniles frequent shallower water. Being the flatfish that they are, halibut prefer to partially

Halibut: fresh (available from March to November); frozen; steaks; fillets; roasts; loins; and other shapely portions

Atlantic Halibut →

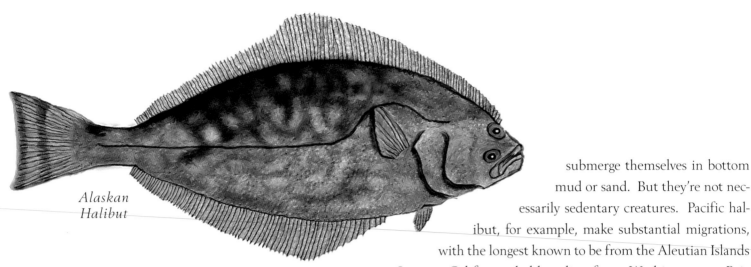

Alaskan Halibut

fish names

Alaska Halibut
(H. stenolepsis):
Pacific halibut

California Halibut
(P. californicus):
Pacific halibut,
California flounder

Atlantic Halibut
(H. hippoglossus)

submerge themselves in bottom mud or sand. But they're not necessarily sedentary creatures. Pacific halibut, for example, make substantial migrations, with the longest known to be from the Aleutian Islands to Oregon. California halibut live from Washington to Baja California, with larger concentrations from Bodega Bay southward. This particular species, common beyond the surfline, seems to follow schools of anchovy, preferring, it seems, the more structured habitats of kelp beds, rocks, and artificial reefs, than its brethren. All the halibuts eat small fish, squid, octopus, shrimps, and other crustaceans. And likewise they're eaten by seals, sea lions, sharks, and large rays.

How They're Doing: Once abundant, Atlantic halibut are now commercially extinct. That is, there are so few of them they're essentially not worth fishing for. Commercial fishing for them began in the early 1820s, but there were early signs of susceptibility to depletion. Shortly after various offshore regions were targeted for halibut—for example from Cape Cod to Stellwagen Bank, Georges Bank, and Nantucket Shoals—fleets were forced to go further offshore to find them plentiful. "The history, in short, of the halibut fishery," wrote Bigelow and Schroeder in 1953, "leaves no doubt that this species shows the effect of hard fishing sooner than most sea fish, it being possible to catch the majority of the stock on any limited area in a few years."

HOW THEY'RE CAUGHT: No commercial fishing is allowed for Atlantic halibut in the U.S., but managers allow boats to bring these fish in as by-kill, and to be caught recreationally. However, scientists insist that for these fish to recover, catching them should be prohibited entirely.

Pacific halibut are managed jointly by a U.S.-Canadian commission that sets quotas and sponsors research. Since 1995, the Pacific catch has been specifically allocated each year among a set of individual vessels who buy and sell shares of the quota. This put an end to what had been a dangerous "derby" fishery, with thousands of boats racing to take the allowed catch in two 24-hour periods, often in hazardous weather. The fishery is now conducted year-round at a much saner pace. Fishing for California halibut is managed by the state with size restrictions, seasons, and catch limits. They're mostly caught using gillnets, but they are also taken on longlines and with trawls in special areas designated for those gear types.

**NUTRITION:
HALIBUT**

110 calories
20 fat calories
2 g total fat
35 mg cholesterol
23 g protein

*(Based on a 3 oz. serving
size. Vitamins and
minerals are based on
2,000 calorie diet.)*

In contrast, Pacific halibut are robust with their abundance considered fairly high relative to historic levels. Likewise, California halibut remain relatively abundant and stable.

Special Issues: So few exist, Atlantic halibut are now merely rare by-kill in New England's fisheries for cod and flounder. In the Alaska longline fishery, there is little by-kill because commercial fishers are able to target their efforts where the fish are and when (see "How They're Caught"). An interesting and successful conservation management measure in Alaska's other groundfish and crab fisheries is that they're shut down if their by-kill of halibut reaches a set limit. Also, Alaska longliners asked for regulations requiring them to use scare devices to prevent albatrosses from getting hooked—a big plus.

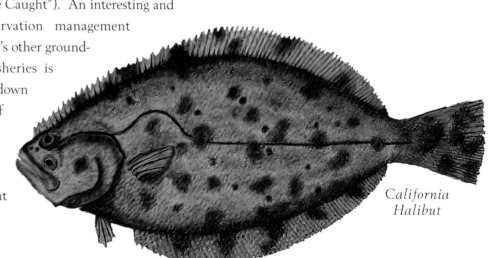

*California
Halibut*

"The history of the halibut in the Gulf of Maine, like that of the salmon, must be written largely in the past-tense for their numbers have been sadly depleted there by overfishing."

Bigelow and Schroeder, 1953

WORLD FISH CONSUMPTION

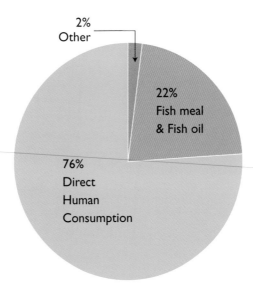

2%
Other

22%
Fish meal
& Fish oil

76%
Direct
Human
Consumption

WORLD FISH OIL PRODUCTION

(sardines, anchovies, herring, menhaden, by products of
pollock and whiting, and by-kill of other fisheries)

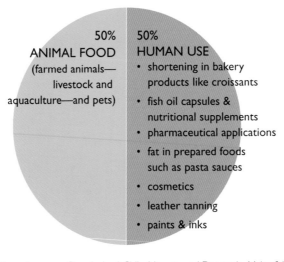

50%
ANIMAL FOOD
(farmed animals—
livestock and
aquaculture—and pets)

50%
HUMAN USE
• shortening in bakery
  products like croissants
• fish oil capsules &
  nutritional supplements
• pharmaceutical applications
• fat in prepared foods
  such as pasta sauces
• cosmetics
• leather tanning
• paints & inks

Major fish oil producers are Peru, Iceland, Chile, Norway, and Denmark. Major fish oil
importers are the Netherlands, Norway, Japan, United Kingdom, Mexico, and Germany.
The U.S. both produces and imports fish oil, but much less so than other nations.

Court Jesters

Pacific Rockfish • Croakers • Groupers • Snappers
Hoki, Roughy, Dory • Patagonian Toothfish

INGREDIENTS

Sundried tomato pesto

3 ounces sundried toma-
toes
1 TBSP minced garlic
⅓ cup loosely packed
  basil leaves
1 TBSP balsamic vinegar
2 TBSP olive oil
2 TBSP water
sea salt and freshly ground
  black pepper

Rosemary polenta

4 tsp olive oil
1 tsp chopped shallots
½ tsp chopped garlic
2 ¼ cup water
½ tsp minced rosemary
  needles
½ tsp sea salt
freshly ground black pep-
per
4 ounces instant Italian
  polenta

*Grilled striped bass &
broccoli rabe*

Four 1 pound whole
striped
  bass, scaled, gutted, and
  cleaned or four 6 ounce
  striped bass fillets
2 TBSP olive oil
sea salt and freshly
  ground black pepper
¾ pound broccoli rabe,
  trimmed

Note: *Striped bass can
be used as a substitute
fish for many of the
depleted species covered
in this chapter.*

Grilled Whole Striped Bass with Sundried Tomato Pesto, Grilled Polenta, & Broccoli Rabe

Sundried tomato pesto: Sundried tomatoes come dry-packed or oil-packed. If you are using dry-pack sundried tomatoes, put them in a small strainer and dip them into boiling water for about 1 minute or until they are softened. Drain the softened tomatoes well before proceeding. This step is not necessary if you use sundried tomatoes preserved in oil.

Put the tomatoes, garlic, basil, vinegar, olive oil, and water into the blender. Purée with an on and off motion until the mixture is chopped. Season to taste with salt and pepper.

Rosemary polenta: Put 3 tsp of the olive oil into a medium saucepan and sauté the shallots and garlic for about 1 minute or until softened. Add the water, rosemary, and salt and pepper to taste. Bring to a boil and stir in the polenta. Cook for 2 minutes, stirring continuously, or until all the water has been absorbed and the polenta is smooth.

Rinse an 8-inch square or round pan with cold water to prevent the polenta from sticking to it. Pour in the polenta and smooth the surface with a wet spatula. Refrigerate. When the polenta is cool and firm, un-mold it and cut into 2 to 3-inch wide strips.

Preheat the grill or broiler.

Brush the polenta with the remaining olive oil and grill 2 to 3 minutes per side until warmed through and marked by the grill. Cut the polenta into wedges or triangles and keep warm in a slow oven.

Grilled striped bass & broccoli rabe: Preheat the grill or broiler. Brush the 4 whole striped bass or fillets with 1 TBSP of the olive oil and season to taste with salt and pepper.

Grill or broil the whole fish for 6 to 8 minutes on the first side or until the flesh in the stomach cavity turns opaque. Turn and grill or broil the other side for about 6 minutes. If you are using fillets, put the skinned side of the fillet toward the heat source. The fillets will take less time to cook than the whole fish, about 4 minutes on each side.

Blanch the broccoli rabe in boiling water or steam it in a medium saucepan using a collapsible steamer until it is tender and bright green, about 3 to 4 minutes. Drain and toss with 1 TBSP of the olive oil. Season to taste with salt and pepper.

Assembly: Divide the broccoli rabe among 4 warm, preferably oval, dinner plates. Place the whole striped bass or one fillet on top of the greens on each plate. Add a spoonful of sundried tomato pesto and 3 or 4 triangles of grilled polenta to the side of each plate.

Contributed by Nora Pouillon, Executive Chef and Owner of Restaurant Nora and Asia Nora, both located in Washington, DC. Restaurant Nora is the first certified organic restaurant in the country.

Yellowtail Rockfish

Pacific Rockfish

Fish Scale

OVERALL RECOMMENDATION:

RED on the Fish Scale, even though some Pacific rockfish may still be abundant, because many are overfished, much remains unknown about them, they're indistinguishable in the market place, and they're highly vulnerable to over-exploitation.

In the Wild: Pacific rockfish come from the genus *Sebastes*, which is from the Greek meaning "magnificent." And magnificent they are. It's a large group, with 60 species so far identified in the Pacific (not counting two in the Atlantic which are not covered in this volume), from the Bering Sea to Baja California. Ever feel like you were adopted into the family whose name you carry because the other members are so unlike you? If they could, Pacific rockfish might feel the same way, as there's such variability in the characteristics among different species in this tribe. Only a few species are described here.

Pacific rockfish inhabit a range of depths and come in all sizes and colors. Some species, like the **yellowtail rockfish**, swim in schools; others are loners, like the **yelloweye rockfish**. Some stay deep, others come close to shore. Some are active during the day, others at night. They do have in common their deep body, spiky fins, and bony cheeks. In general, Pacific rockfish spend a good deal of time resting close to the ocean bottom but rise into the water column to feed. As juveniles some visit the intertidal zone, rising with the tide to feed and, ironically, to escape predation only to frequently meet their fate at the ends of anglers' lines (see below). They live long lives, from 20 to 100 years or more, depending on the species, and, of course, whether they're caught before then. Interestingly, some rockfish species give birth to live young; others lay eggs.

Take **Pacific Ocean perch** for example. Their size of 20 inches belies the fact that they can live to 90 years. To procreate, they must be fertilized internally, and when it's time, the females

 Pacific Rockfish: whole; dressed; fillets; frozen; sushi and sashimi

Pacific Rockfish

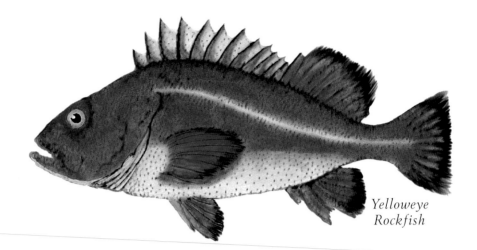

Yelloweye Rockfish

fish names

Pacific Ocean Perch
(S. alutus)

Yelloweye Rockfish
(S. ruberrimus)

Bocaccio *(S. paucispinis)*

Widow Rockfish
(S. entomelas):
brownie rockfish

Yellowtail Rockfish
(S.favidus): greenie
rockfish

Pacific Rockfish *(Sebastes
spp):* red snapper (not to
be confused with the real
red snapper, *L. campechanu,*
of the Gulf of Mexico), rock
cod, Pacific snapper, also,
not to be confused with
the East Coast regional
name of rockfish for
striped bass

deliver live young. In *Fish: An Enthusiast's Guide*, a joyful study of living fishes, Peter Moyle relates that, "When such fishes are nearly ready to give birth, the young may occupy an amazing amount of room and seriously impair the ability of the female to swim." A frightening prospect indeed. Pacific Ocean perch are bright red on the back, and silvery underneath and occur from Japan and the Bering Sea all the way to Baja California. They're usually found at about 600 feet, but deeper than 2,700 feet is not altogether uncommon.

Widow rockfish are found from Kodiak to southern Baja California usually around reefs. Most adults are found between 150 and 1,000 feet deep. They can live nearly 60 years and grow two feet long. Since they're most active at night, they for a long time avoided being discovered and caught by commercial fishers who worked mostly in daylight hours. But 'tis a thing of the past. **Yelloweye rockfish** has the distinction of being one of the larger, longer-living rockfish, growing three feet and somehow living more than a century. **Boccacio** also grows to three feet but has a shorter, yet still impressive, life-span of about 35 years.

How They're Doing: Overall they're doing poorly, principally because they're slow-growing, long-lived, and there's a lot of fishing pressure on them by both U.S. and foreign boats. Pacific Ocean perch, bocaccio, and canary rockfish are definitely depleted. But managers have ranked some rockfish species as being healthy

**NUTRITION:
OCEAN PERCH**

110 calories
25 fat calories
3.5 g total fat
75 mg cholesterol
20 g protein
Calcium 4%

(Based on a 3 oz. serving size. Vitamins and minerals are based on 2,000 calorie diet.)

HOW THEY'RE CAUGHT: Pacific Ocean perch, yelloweye rockfish, bocaccio, widow, and yellowtail are caught the most and have the highest value among West Coast rockfish fishes, even though a number of them are depleted and continue to decline. Fishers use trawl, other types of net gear, traps, or hook and line gear to catch Pacific rockfish. Some species are favored by anglers, and in areas of Puget Sound some local populations are depleted from recreational catches.

enough to continue fishing for, including most from Alaskan waters, such as widow rockfish, chilipepper rockfish, and yellowtail rockfish. The status of many other rockfish remains unknown. Several species of rockfish off the coast of Washington not covered here are being considered for listing under the Endangered Species Act.

As varied as the Pacific rockfish family is, different species are frequently caught together, meaning that while fishers may try to catch one species of rockfish in trawl gear or other non-elective gear, they'll inevitably pull up other rockfish species as well. So even if a species is known to be in trouble, it's hard for fishers to avoid catching them. (The exception is Pacific Ocean perch which seem to congregate together among themselves but not with other rock-fishes.) Also, because the depth at which they're caught—frequently very deep—it's impossible to return the unwanted ones to the sea because they're essentially dead, or close to dead, as their swim bladders expand so much while being brought to the surface quickly, forcing their stomachs out their mouths and their eyes to bulge.

**NUTRITION:
PACIFIC ROCKFISH**
(Sebastes)

100 calories
20 fat calories
2.0 g total fat
40 mg cholesterol
21 g protein

(Based on a 3 oz. serving size. Vitamins and minerals are based on 2,000 calorie diet.)

Bocaccio

On Eating Them:

The red-skinned fish fetch higher prices than those colored or duller, encouraging marketers to sell their goods as "red snapper." California allows Pacific Ocean perch and other red-skinned rockfish to be marketed in that state as "Pacific snapper," however the Food and Drug Administration prohibits any other fish besides the red snapper of Gulf of Mexico origin to be sold as "red snapper." (Look for the other real red snapper in the snapper section, beginning on page 39.)

**LONGEVITY OF VARIOUS
PACIFIC ROCKFISHES**

Pacific Ocean Perch — 90 years	
Widow Rockfish — 60 years	
Yellowtail Rockfish — 64 years	
Yelloweye Rockfish — 100 years	
Bocaccio — 35 years	

*Widow
Rockfish*

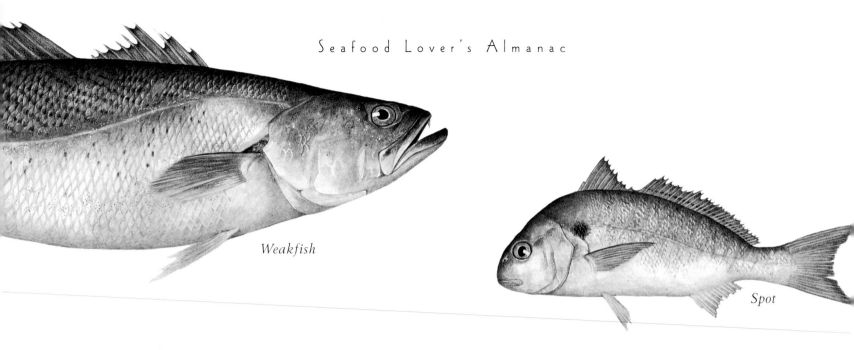

Weakfish

Spot

Croaker Clan

Fish Scale

These fall in the YELLOW to RED zone on Audubon's Fish Scale.

In the Wild: Members of this large and varied family *(Sciaenidae)* got their name of "croakers" and "drums" because of their noisy habit of vibrating muscles attached to their swim bladders produce a thrumming, booming noise. The few members of the clan who don't have swim bladders to make up for the lack by grinding their teeth. Some believe this sound relates to courtship and spawning. Others think it can also be a fear response, as they croak a lot when they're caught and presumably quite scared.

Most of the croaker clan live in the south Atlantic and Gulf of Mexico, usually near shore in muddy bays and estuaries where they feed on shrimps, oysters, crabs, invertebrates, and fishes. **Weakfish** frequent northern waters in the mid-Atlantic as well. Weakfish used to grow to about three feet and more than 15 pounds, but nowadays you're unlikely to find one bigger than two feet long and six pounds.

Palm-sized, **spot** are so-named for the dark spot behind the eye. The giant **black drum** grows to over four feet and 100 pounds. In addition to having small, pointy jaw teeth, black drum also grow large fat flat teeth in their throat with which to crush the shellfish they eat.

How They're Doing: Croakers, drums, and related fishes in the southeast Atlantic and Gulf of Mexico are at their lowest population levels in history, but they have a tremendous capacity to recover if given the chance. Red drum, which were targeted heavily during the Cajun food craze for "blackened red-fish," are severely overfished. So much so that the federal government now prohibits commercial fishing for them in federal waters. In the mid-

fish names

Atlantic Croaker
(M. undulatus)

Black Drum
(P. cromis)

Red Drum
(S. ocellatus): red-fish, channel bass

Spot *(L. xanthurus)*

Weakfish *(C. regalis):* sea trout

Weakfish
Red Drum
Black Drum

Spot

Croaker: canned pet food; processed animal feed; fresh whole fish; frozen whole fishsteaks; frozen fillets; precooked breaded fillets.

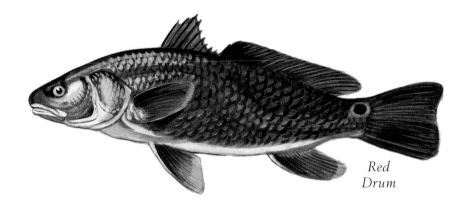

Red
Drum

Atlantic, weakfish seem to be coming back after new restrictions limited winter fishing on juveniles.

Special Issues: The croaker clan, including large numbers of juvenile spot, become victims of by-kill in shrimp trawl nets. Before fish excluder devices started to be used in shrimp nets in the late 1990s, trawlers dumped billions of spot, croaker, and drum every year.

Black
Drum

On Eating Them: Health officials recommend not eating croakers and drum raw because they frequently harbor a certain parasite harmful to humans. But take heart, the parasites are killed when cooked.

Markets: The U.S. both imports and exports numerous species of the croaker clan. Mexico also exports them. Spot are caught by anglers as a food fish and they're also marketed whole as a pan fish. Most of the spot caught commercially goes to pet food.

HOW THEY'RE CAUGHT: Croakers are a favored target of inshore recreational anglers because they frequent shallow estuaries. The principal commercial use of croaker, spot, and other species in this group is as raw material for the pet food industry. Recreational fishers take about the same amount of black and red drums, Atlantic croaker, and weakfish as the commercial fishers. In fact, in many states rimming the Gulf of Mexico, regulations favor recreational catch of these fish. Most commercial fishing for Atlantic croaker occurs in the Gulf of Mexico, Mississippi Delta, and the Chesapeake Bay, where fishers catch them with gillnets, pound nets, hook and line, and fish traps. Drum are mostly gillnetted and occasionally taken in seines. Since most drum and croaker occur in nearshore waters, the states manage fishing for them. Another management issue that clouds the fishing pressure these fishes face is that the fish caught for pet food are reported in a lump sum labeled "industrial fishery catch," so managers don't know how many are taken of which species.

HOW TO CHOOSE YOUR SEAFOOD

The following rules for your own safety come from the National Fisheries Institute:

1. Know your fishmonger. Buy seafood products only from reputable dealers.

2. Look for fish with bright, clear eyes, scales that cling to the skin, bright pink gills, and a mild sea breeze odor. Check for unscarred skin that springs back to the touch.

3. At the market, make sure cooked seafood products do not come in contact with uncooked or raw seafood in the same case.

4. Always cook fish thoroughly to an internal temperature of 145 degrees.

5. If in doubt about any seafood, pass it by.

*Nassau
Grouper*

Grouper Tribe

In the Wild: A large tribe with many species, groupers are essentially tropical fishes, extending into the sub-tropics and occasionally temperate seas (Florida Keys, Gulf of Mexico, Bahamas, throughout the Caribbean, Indo-Pacific...). In general, they are loners except when the urge to breed comes upon them. Then they gather in famously large groups to spawn, the timing and location of which are remarkably predictable (many times occurring around specific moon phases). Sometimes these gatherings include as many as 100,000 individuals capable of producing billions of eggs. It is then that groupers from a large area are most vulnerable. Recent findings from researchers indicate that some groupers return from their wide wanderings to spawn in the very area they themselves were born.

**OVERALL
RECOMMENDATION:**

Groupers are deep in the RED on the Fish Scale. Pass up that grouper sandwich and ask for mahimahi instead. Also, farmed tilapia can substitute for grouper.

Groupers vary from the tiniest denizens of the underside of reefs to the giant **jewfish** that can be as large as a Volkswagen (eight feet, 780 pounds, but nowadays they're much smaller). Many groupers live for decades, some of them for 40 years or more, possibly longer than any other reef species. As adults they dwell among reefs or other underwater structures like wrecks, while juveniles often spend their time inshore in seagrass beds. They feed on fish, crabs, and squid mostly. Jewfish have a bigger appetite, turning to turtles, stingrays, and the like. Although the grouper shape has been described as "typical fish," their colors make up for their lack of other adornment: from red to yellow to violet to black, with spots and stripes that go from white to black and back again.

Groupers: live; whole fish; sashimi; fresh; fillets; breaded fillets; breaded grouper "cheeks" sometimes served in sandwiches

Most groupers (Nassau grouper being an exception) change sex as they age, beginning life as females and changing to males as they grow larger. This is called hermaphroditism (having the ability to change sex). Most hermaphroditic populations have more females than males. Females prefer larger males. So do fishers (but more on that below).

The **Nassau grouper** can live 28 years, maturing at about six years old. They are notorious among divers as easy to approach. Alan Davidson, in *Seafood: A Connoisseur's Guide and Cookbook,* recounts the story of one of these fish literally picking the pockets of an underwater photographer who had stored them full of crayfish tails. In contrast, the **black grouper** is skittish. And jewfishes have been known to stalk and attempt to nibble divers. No doubt all have distinguished personalities.

Nassau Grouper
(E. striatus)

Black Grouper
(M. bonaci): not to be confused with the misty grouper *(E. mystacinus)*, also called black grouper and from the West Atlantic

Jewfish *(E. itajara)*: giant grouper, spotted jewfish

Red Grouper *(E. morio)*

...and many others

How They're Doing: Groupers include some of the most highly valued fish of tropical and sub-tropical reefs. They are sold both alive (with some species fetching more than US $50/pound) and dead. Unfortunately, groupers are also distinguished as being among the most susceptible of reef fish when subjected to even moderate fishing pressure. Fishers tend to target the bigger ones. In hermaphroditic fish, this has ripple effects on future generations: the loss of males can drop so low that little successful fertilization can be achieved, as has been seen with the gag grouper in the Gulf of Mexico.

Indeed, from some areas, populations have virtually disappeared and more than 15 groupers are now included on the World Conservation Union's Red List of Threatened Animals. "Throughout its range," writes Carl Safina in his book *Song for the Blue Ocean,* almost a third of all the Nassau grouper's spawning aggregations have disappeared. ... [In] Honduras, where ten thousand

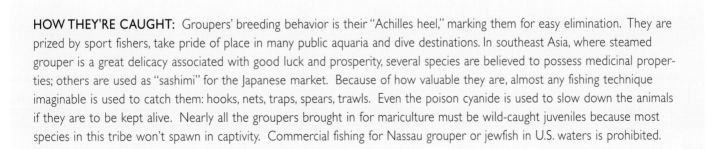

Jewfish

HOW THEY'RE CAUGHT: Groupers' breeding behavior is their "Achilles heel," marking them for easy elimination. They are prized by sport fishers, take pride of place in many public aquaria and dive destinations. In southeast Asia, where steamed grouper is a great delicacy associated with good luck and prosperity, several species are believed to possess medicinal properties; others are used as "sashimi" for the Japanese market. Because of how valuable they are, almost any fishing technique imaginable is used to catch them: hooks, nets, traps, spears, trawls. Even the poison cyanide is used to slow down the animals if they are to be kept alive. Nearly all the groupers brought in for mariculture must be wild-caught juveniles because most species in this tribe won't spawn in captivity. Commercial fishing for Nassau grouper or jewfish in U.S. waters is prohibited.

Black Grouper

Red Grouper

fish had spawned at a newly discovered site one year earlier, five hundred breeding fish were counted in 1991." Not surprisingly, two species, the jewfish and the Nassau grouper, were among the few fully-marine fishes ever proposed for Endangered Species Act listing in the U.S. (But they have never actually been listed.) Jewfish are so depleted there's a "WANTED" poster out for them calling on divers and fishers to report any of these fish they might see.

Groupers in general are classified as either fully exploited or overfished in the Caribbean, the Gulf of Mexico, western central Atlantic, Mediterranean, and Indo-Pacific, yet world catches of them continue to increase.

Special Issues: Because groupers are often caught with wire traps that continue to kill if lost ("ghost-fishing"), by-kill can be high. By-kill is also high in trawl or on longline gear. Many species come from deep water and are already injured (or dead) when brought to the surface, so there's poor survival of undersized fish when released.

Markets: Exporters of grouper are the U.S., Mexico, Brazil, Venezuela, Argentina, South Africa, Indonesia, and southeast Asia. Primary consumers are the U.S., Japan, Hong Kong, France, Spain, Portugal, and Italy.

"What is happening to groupers worldwide should act as a warning, like we have seen in cod, that fishery management is a necessity not a luxury, and that even the production of millions of eggs provides no safeguard in the absence of good management."

– *Yvonne Sadovy, Ph.D., University of Hong Kong*

*Vermilion
Snapper*

*Yellowtail
Snapper*

*Silk
Snapper*

Snappers

**OVERALL
RECOMMENDATION:**

*Most snappers fall in the RED on
the Fish Scale because they're depleted, poorly managed, and have high by-
kill associated with them. We put yellowtail snapper in the YELLOW as a
precaution because its status is uncertain. Avoiding Gulf of Mexico
shrimp helps red snappers.*

There is only one fish allowed to be marketed as "red snapper" in the United States, and
that is the species *L. campechanus.* You can recognize it by its bright red-pink back,
and pink belly, usually with its skin on for this very reason. Don't confuse this fish
with redfish, which is also called red drum (see page 34), or Pacific red snapper (see
page 32). The other true "red snapper" is a southern cousin (*L. purpureus*), occurring only in the Caribbean. The two are extremely similar, and some biologists consider them separate races of the same species. In the northeast U.S., "snapper" refers
to baby bluefish, something else entirely.

In the Wild: Snappers are found around the world in the tropics and subtropics.
They are either associated with deep-water reefs, rocky ledges (red, blackfin, silk, vermilion,
yellowtail), or shallow nearshore areas such as bays, shallow reefs, tidal creeks, and mangrove
sloughs (gray, and occasionally mutton). Like other reef fishes, snappers grow slowly and live
for many years, some growing quite large—the cubera snapper, for example, can bulk up to 100
pounds. Many species, however, grow to be two feet and 25 pounds; yet many others are
smaller, like the school master and yellowtail snappers.

Red and **yellowtail snappers** move around in small schools with their kin. Red snappers prefer to cruise near the bottom, anywhere from about 60 to 400 feet, with older populations of
larger sized fish choosing cooler, deeper spots. They spawn offshore, but little else is known of
their spawning habits or their very early stages of life. The young are scattered throughout
coastal areas over muddy and muddy-sand bottom, where they feed on small crustaceans.

Yellowtail
Snapper

Red Snapper: whole fresh fish; frozen; often with the skin on
Snapper is also sold as "fingers," lengths of boneless, skinless meat

All other
Snappers

fish names

Silk Snapper
(*L. vivanus*)

Red Snapper
(*L. campechanus*)

Yellowtail Snapper
(*O. chrysurus*)

Vermilion Snapper
(*R. aurorubens*)

Mutton Snapper
(*L. analis*)

...and 180 others

fish fact

The yellowtail you'll find in sushi bars is the Pacific yellowtail, an unrelated species to the yellowtail snapper profiled here.

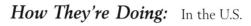

Red Snapper

Adult red snappers feed on a variety of fish and invertebrates, as the occasion dictates.

How They're Doing:

In the U.S. South Atlantic and Gulf of Mexico, red snapper is depleted and vermilion snapper is nearly overfished.

The status of yellowtail snapper is unknown, as is the status of many snapper species. There are fewer snappers in the Caribbean than there were historically. A number of snapper populations in New Zealand are declining and believed to be below what's needed to sustain fishing at current levels.

Special Issues:

Much of the habitat important to juvenile snappers in the Gulf of Mexico has been degraded by pollution and development. By-kill of juvenile snappers in shrimp trawls is a major problem.

On Eating Them:

Ciguetera is a rare type of poisoning that occurs in tropical fish like snappers in certain areas at some times of the year. The toxin usually occurs in larger fish, and is dangerous to humans. The toxin can be avoided by not buying fish from reefs known to have ciguatera.

Markets:

The main consumers of snapper are the U.S., Mexico, Europe, and South America. Big exporters are Mexico, Venezuela, Brazil, U.S., Caribbean countries, Thailand, Taiwan, Philippines.

HOW THEY'RE CAUGHT: Snappers are a favorite target of recreational anglers the world over, taken with every gear from spears to handlines to the best rig a charter boat has to offer. Regarded as some of the best eating fishes, they have been caught for local consumption by many native inhabitants throughout the tropics, as well as for market. Management is skimpy in many of the areas where snappers are taken, with little monitoring of catch and few management measures in place.

In the U.S., where managers in the Gulf of Mexico, Caribbean, and South Atlantic regions set official catch and size limits, the recovery of the depleted red snapper population is still frustrated by high mortality of juvenile snappers in shrimp trawls and consistent quota busting by recreational fishers, who take half the catch.

Hoki

Hoki, Orange Roughy, Oreo Dory

OVERALL RECOMMENDATION:

Okey dokey if it's hoki, but it's a different story for oreo dory and orange roughy. Orange roughy are slow to recover from overfishing, and oreo dory are the collateral damage of that enterprise. These both rate RED on the Fish Scale. Even though these deepwater species are caught together, the hoki is doing better because of its different lifestyle and abundance, and falls in the YELLOW/ GREEN section of the Fish Scale. Catfish can substitute for orange roughy.

In the Wild: **Hoki** comes from the Maori meaning "to return." It's found in deep water (600 to 2,500 feet) off New Zealand and southern Australia. Belonging to the hake family, it is long and thin with blue-green, silvery sides and a sharply pointed tail. Growing to three feet long, it can weigh up to three pounds.

Orange roughy isn't really orange until after it's caught and dies. The live fish is reddish with iridescent blue on the belly. This species is found in deep water off New Zealand, Australia, and Namibia, and in small numbers off Iceland, Scotland, and the Canadian maritimes. Orange roughy grow slowly and reproduce late in life. They can live a full 150 years and don't mature until they're about 30 years old. They congregate in large groups during spawning around seamounts, which are underwater mountains. They grow to 16 inches long and weigh about three pounds.

Oreo dory also live long lives and grow slowly, and in fact are found in the same areas and habitats as orange roughy. Oreo dory weigh only as much as two pounds and can grow to two feet long, but more typically they're half that size.

How They're Doing: Hoki are abundant off New Zealand, but orange roughy and oreo dory are not. Many populations were severely overfished when the fishery took off in the early 1980s. Recovery will likely require decades because they're long-lived and mature late in

Hoki: frozen fillets; surimi; fish sticks; fish and chips; nuggets; and smoked fillets
Orange Roughy: always frozen fillets in the U.S; oil used in cosmetics
Oreo Dory: frozen skinless fillets

Hoki

Orange Roughy

Oreo Dory

Orange Roughy

NUTRITION: ORANGE ROUGHY

80 calories
10 fat calories
total fat 1.0 g
20 mg cholesterol
16 g protein

(Based on a 3 oz. serving size. Vitamins and minerals are based on 2,000 calorie diet.)

life. Orange roughy is still on menus and seafood counters only because fishers have moved on to newly discovered (though much smaller) populations.

Special Issues: By-kill is a significant problem in these deepwater trawl fisheries, where all the species are caught as a group. Oreo dory initially was by-kill of the orange roughy fishery, but now is targeted since roughy catches continue to decline. In addition, dragging trawl gear over seamounts and pinnacles causes serious damage to habitat.

Oreo Dory

Markets: The U.S. is the principal importer of orange roughy and hoki, while Australia follows second for orange roughy, and is the main consumer of oreo dory, with Japan a close second. Canada, Germany, and France also serve these fish. Hoki is the most valuable export fish species for New Zealand, and orange roughy is its number three export.

Hoki *(M. novaezelandiae)*: blue hake, New Zealand whiting, blue grenedier

Orange Roughy
(H. atlanticus)

Oreo Dory
(A. niger)

HOW THEY'RE CAUGHT: Fishing for hoki, orange roughy, and oreo dory occurs year-round with trawl gear at great depths in the southern and sub-Antarctic waters off New Zealand and off southern Australia. In an attempt to control fishing in the 1980s, New Zealand created a system that awarded quota shares of several species to individual companies. In its early days, officials had little life history information on these species and overestimated how many fish there were. This led to rapid overfishing, especially for orange roughy. These fish are easy to catch because they congregate in large groups to spawn. At the height of fishing, five to 12 million individual orange roughy were removed from their spawning grounds each year. Adjustments over the years have improved the system, but concerns remain that they're still not adequate to bring back the fish.

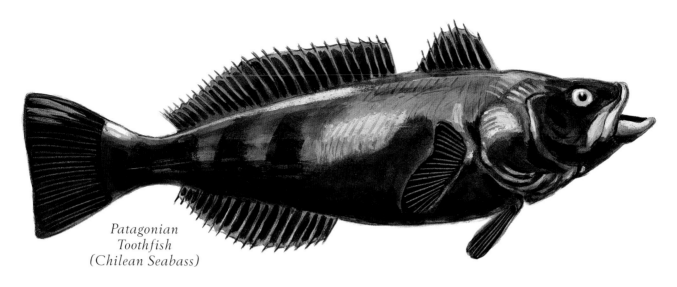

*Patagonian
Toothfish
(Chilean Seabass)*

Patagonian Toothfish

**OVERALL
RECOMMENDATION:**

*No doubt this one falls in the
RED zone on the Fish Scale. It is
the target of rampant fishing in the
waters around Antarctica. It's overfished, with high by-kill of albatrosses and petrels, and most of
the catch is taken illegally.*

In the Wild: A denizen of the cold and deep, this species lives in sub-Antarctic waters around the Southern Ocean (that's the area around Antarctica where the southern extremes of the Atlantic, Pacific, and Indian oceans meet). Scientists don't know much beyond the basics about this species. Slender and dark-silver in color, the Patagonian toothfish can grow to more than six feet long and up to 100 pounds. A relatively slow-growing, long-lived species, the Patagonian toothfish first matures and begins to spawn after 10 or 12 years old, and can live a hearty 50 years. They frequent nutrient-rich banks near land along the continental shelf, sea mounts, and along ice shelves, and feed mainly on squid, amphipods, and prawns. Sperm whales eat them and scientists estimate that they comprise up to 98 percent of the diet of elephant seals.

How They're Doing: Scientists say the population of Patagonian toothfish could soon collapse and they predict commercial extinction before 2005. Even with increasing fishing effort, catches continue to decline and the fish landed are smaller and smaller—both signs of a population in trouble.

fish fact

Chilean seabass is a
market pseudonym
for the Patagonian
toothfish.

On Eating Them: Chilean seabass is *not* the same fish as Patagonian toothfish as some marketers would have you believe. Patagonian toothfish is called Chilean seabass to mask illegal catches and trade. The best way to tell them apart in the market or on menus is price. Seabass is an average-priced white flesh fish, while toothfish is notably more expensive. And, their tastes are distinguishable from one another. It is safe to say that most of what appears in the markets is actually toothfish, not seabass.

Patagonian Toothfish: skinless frozen fillets frequently sold as Chilean seabass

Fish
Scale

Patagonian
Toothfish

Patagonian Toothfish

D. eleginoides): Chilean seabass, seabass, Chilean grouper, black hake, Antarctic cod, icefish, mero (in Japan)

Special Issues: The areas fished are so remote that vast areas are never policed, resulting in a great deal of illegal fishing. There is high bycatch associated with catching toothfish, including albatrosses, petrels, as well as other fish. (Albatrosses dive to catch the bait on hooks, get hooked, and they're pulled down and drowned.) This problem is so severe that it threatens some albatross and petrel populations with extinction.

Markets: The Patagonian toothfish rose in the marketplace when supplies of other white-fleshed fish such as orange roughy dwindled. Most is exported to Japan, the U.S., and Europe.

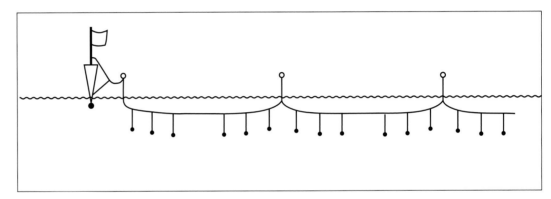

Longlines with baited hooks, kept at the desired depth by spaced floats (for drift longlines) or held to the bottom with weights (bottom longlines). Longlines can be miles long and contain thousands of hooks.

HOW THEY'RE CAUGHT: Fishers primarily use longlines to catch Patagonian toothfish in waters from 1,200 feet to more than two miles deep. Unregulated and illegal catches of toothfish are the main threats to this vulnerable species. Antarctic-Treaty countries manage a portion of the Patagonian toothfish fishery in those waters and around subantarctic islands. In addition, fishing occurs within Chilean and Argentinian waters. The countries who make decisions about fishing around Antarctica began to set quotas for the fish starting in 1994, although they did this with little information on the size of the toothfish population or the effects of fishing on this species. Though they are obligated to conserve species, they have little authority or ability to enforce their decisions. This is in large part because the quotas only apply to those nations which are members of the Antarctic Fisheries Convention and most of the vessels involved evade regulations by re-registering, or "flagging," themselves under another non-member country. The extent of the problem is enormous: an excess of 100,000 tons of illegally caught fish flooded onto the market in 1998-1999. The legal limit was 10,500 tons.

Creepy Crawlers
Lobsters • Crabs

American Lobster

Lobsters

In the Wild: The American, or Maine, lobster can be found from Labrador to Cape Hatteras, in rocky or mud bottom coastal areas. They also occur near deep submarine canyons along the edge of the continental shelf. This denizen of cool waters has 10 legs and two powerful claws—one for crushing and one for ripping or cutting up its food. In their full, living glory, they are greenish-brown with black spots, but come in other colors depending on where they reside. (They only turn red after they're cooked!) While small lobsters don't move around much, studies show that the larger animals travel extensively. Before they were heavily fished, **American lobsters** used to grow to magnificent sizes and live great ages. For example, one caught off the Virginia coast in the 1930s was more than three feet long and weighed 45 pounds. Now they more typically weigh a mere three pounds. As lobsters grow, they molt (shed their shell) repeatedly. Each molt ups their fecundity (fertility): the older, bigger females carry more eggs. Lobsters don't begin maturing until they're about seven years old, and if luck is on their side, they can live 40 years. Unfortunately, that's not likely in the current climate of lobster mania.

Similar to crabs, lobsters mate after the female molts, and then she carries the eggs under her abdomen for about 10 months, hatching them in the late spring and early summer. According to scientists, at the legal minimum size, a mere four to 23 percent of females along

OVERALL RECOMMENDATION:

American and California spiny lobsters rate a YELLOW on Audubon's Fish Scale. While they're inherently vulnerable to overfishing and natural changes to their environment, American ("Maine") lobsters and California spiny lobsters are fairly abundant, and caught with little by-kill. Caribbean spiny lobster falls square in the YELLOW because they're not as abundant. Crawfish is a good substitute for lobster.

California Spiny Lobster

American Lobster

Caribbean Spiny Lobster

American, or "Maine" Lobsters: live, whole-cooked; whole-frozen; frozen tails; frozen claws; whole in brine; fresh picked; and canned meat
Spiny Lobsters: live; fresh whole or tails; frozen; or picked meat

Creepy Crawlers

fish names

American Lobster
(H. americanus):
Maine lobster

California Spiny Lobster
(P. interruptus)

Caribbean Spiny Lobster
(P. argus)

Spiny lobsters rub their antennae across their shells, creating a sound reminiscent of creaking of doors in a haunted house.

— *Maryjo Koch,*
Pond Lake River Sea

the U.S. East Coast are capable of producing eggs. At the next molt size, 40 to 52 percent are capable of "egging." A good argument for delayed gastronomic satisfaction.

On the pricklier side of things, there are nearly 50 species of **spiny lobsters**. The Atlantic varieties are usually reddish brown, while their Pacific cousins sport a rather greenish-orange shell. They, of course, get their name from their spiny, spiky shell, which is an evolutionary adaptation to ward off predators. They have 10 legs, long antennae, and no real claws. These animals, too, grow slowly, and require seven to 11 years and dozens of molts to mature. California spiny lobster range from Monterey Bay to Mexico, preferring rocky habitat anywhere from the coastline to more than 240 feet deep. As fully developed spinies they're nocturnal, hiding in rocks by day and foraging at night. Their larvae start out drifting at sea for a year and a half before settling on the bottom and becoming who they're destined to be. Atlantic spiny lobsters are found from North Carolina to Brazil, but more of them concentrate in the tropical waters of Florida and the Caribbean. These animals also molt frequently until they come of age. These spiny lobster larvae may drift at sea for as long as nine months, and the origin of the animals found in Florida could be from Puerto Rico, Cuba, or elsewhere.

How They're Doing:

Most female lobsters are removed before their best spawning years, even though they may be legal to catch. Although American lobsters appear to be abundant in the Northeast, surveys indicate that the lobster population is

*Spiny
Lobster*

ON EATING THEM

The light-green "tomally" in the carapace of the lobster is the liver and pancreas, which accumulate environmental contaminants. Many advise against eating it, others claim it to be a delicacy.

made up of mostly younger animals that have not yet had a chance to reproduce. So, in what may seem a paradox, while being abundant, they're overfished. Lobsters in Long Island Sound succumbed to a disease and the fishery collapsed in late 1999, underscoring the uncertain future of the intensely fished American lobster. Spiny lobsters are overfished in many parts of the tropics. Managers in Florida and Puerto Rico are attempting to reduce catches there. Catches of spiny lobsters from the Caribbean, South America, Africa, and Australia have all been declining since 1980.

Special Issues: Most American lobsters are caught with habitat-friendly, low by-kill traps. However, lobsters elsewhere are victims of by-kill in trawl fisheries. In Puerto Rico, fishers actually use small lobsters as bait to catch bigger spiny lobsters. In some tropical countries, the main by-kill is fishermen themselves who dive with very bad equipment and little training, and often become crippled with decompression sickness.

NUTRITION: LOBSTER

80 calories
5 fat calories
0.5 g total fat
60 mg cholesterol
17 g protein

(Based on a 3 oz. serving size. Vitamins and minerals are based on 2,000 calorie diet.)

fish fact

The number of lobster traps in Maine waters has quadrupled since 1950. It's the region's single most valuable commercial species, accounting for $242.2 million in 1996 and supporting 50,000 jobs.

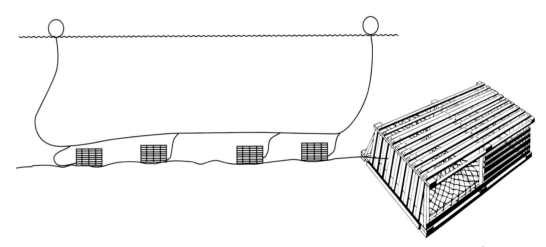

Traps (pots) *are cages or baskets made of wood, wicker, metal rods, wire netting, or other materials for catching fish or crustaceans that enter through one or more openings. The traps are set on the ocean bottom and connected to ropes attached to buoys on the surface.*

HOW THEY'RE CAUGHT: American lobsters are commercially caught both inshore and offshore with baited pots (wire or wooden cages). They're left in the water two or more days before being hauled back on board. Small, illegally sized lobsters are thrown back to live another day, or two, or three... Size limits are strictly enforced, and taking egg-bearing females is verboten. Most commercial lobster fishers work solo or in a small-scale operation.

Fishers catch Caribbean spiny lobsters primarily with fish traps, lobster traps, and by diving for them. A so-called recreational fishery in the Florida Keys has become a greedy grab fest in a two-day opening where more than 100,000 participants race to fill coolers, tubs, and buckets with spiny lobsters, much of which end up being sold. California fishers set rectangular traps that are lobster-friendly, with gear designed to allow undersized animals to escape.

Blue Crab
(male)

Blue Crab
(female)

Crabs

OVERALL RECOMMENDATION:

A varied group, they rate all the way from GREEN to RED on the Fish Scale. Chesapeake Bay blue crabs are overfished and rate a YELLOW, but blue crabs elsewhere are doing well and rate a GREEN. Dungeness crabs are well-managed and fall in the GREEN. Stone crabs rate a GREEN because they're well-managed and abundant. The others—red king crabs, snow crabs, and Tanner crabs—are in the yellow due to low numbers but their fisheries are strictly managed.

In the Wild: There are a few things all these crabs have in common: their five pairs of legs, one of which ends in a set of pincers, their carapace (shell housing), and their start in life as floating larvae in the sea.

Callinectes sapidus (which means "beautiful swimmer") are found in shallow water along the Atlantic coast from Massachusetts to Florida and off the coasts of all the Gulf of Mexico states. They are green-brown with a light underside. **Blue crabs** feed on small fish, clams, mussels, worms, and other detritus, and in turn are eaten by spotted seatrout, red drum, croaker, gars, sheepshead, and fresh and salt water catfish. Herons, diving ducks, and raccoons also eat blue crabs.

A female blue crab undergoes about twenty molts (some call these soft-shell stages "peeler crabs") and mates only once in its at-most two-year lifespan. Because of human intervention and appetite, especially in Chesapeake Bay waters, most only live a year. During their lifetimes, males and females move with surprising agility and determination between salty and fresher water. The male grows bigger (four to six inches across) and has bright blue claws. The front claws on the female are red, which perhaps helps the male find appropriate mates. In calm moments, their eyes look like black little beads. But when on alert, the black beads rise up on stalks—quite handy, as they prefer the soft mud bottoms of

Fish Scale

Blue Crab
Stone Crab
Dungeness Crab →

Chesapeake Bay Blue Crab
Red King Crab
Snow Crab →

Blue Crab: sold as live, whole; picked meat sold fresh; frozen, or canned. Newly molted blue crabs are the "soft shell" crabs on market, available from April through September.
King, Tanner, and Snow Crabs: legs usually frozen; also sold live
Dungeness Crab: live; whole cooked; cooked sections; picked fresh meat; frozen; canned
Stone Crab: claws only
Imitation Crab: surimi made from hake or pollock

Similar to Tanners, king crabs amass in gigantic pod formations to protect themselves from predators. One pod can contain a thousand king crabs!

fish names

Blue Crab *(C. sapidus)*

Dungeness Crab *(C. magister)*

Red King Crab *(P. camtshaticus, P. platypus, L. aequispinus)*

Snow Crab *(C. opilio)*

Tanner Crab *(C. bairdi)*

Stone Crab *(M. mercenaria)*

Jonah Crab *(C. borealis)*

fish fact

Crabs from Asia are being sold as "blue crabs" in the Chesapeake.

King Crab pod

bays and channels near river mouths where they bury themselves to the eyestalks. (If you're inclined to look closely with a magnifying glass, you'll notice their eyes have a vertical stripe.) During mating, which blue crabs do under the protective cover of sea grass patches, a male crab envelops the female and cradle-guards her until her shell cracks and she molts for the very last time. (Don't worry, he doesn't squeeze her too hard, her shell cracks naturally.) Sometimes they have to travel a ways in this cradle-carry position to find the perfect nuptial spot. As if playing a harp, he sensuously moves water with his swimmerets to keep her oxygenated during this vulnerable period. With his gentle assistance, now in her soft phase she turns over on her back so they are belly-to-belly, face-to-face. He deposits his sperm in her sack and guards her for about two more days until her new shell hardens. She goes off to deeper water and, at a time she determines which could be weeks to months later, uses the stored sperm to fertilize her hundreds of thousands of eggs, and the cycle starts anew with another generation.

From Alaska to central California, **dungeness crabs** roam on open sandy bottom or near rocky structures at water's edge (intertidal zone) to as deep as 1,000 feet. Two popular stamping grounds for young dungeness crabs are in Washington's Willapa Bay and Grays Harbor, but all the estuaries along Washington and Oregon are important for *Cancer magister*. *Cancer*, by the way, is Latin for crab. With a light reddish-brown shell and whitish to light orange underside, dungeness crabs mature when their carapace (shell) is about four inches across, a size indicating they're about two years old. But if allowed, they can grow to be a full three pounds and a whole foot across. The abundance of these crabs is cyclical, and their boom and bust cycles seem to be driven by changing ocean currents and winds, since that is how their larvae are distributed.

The fashion fab **king crab** comes in a broad complexion of colors from red (*P. camtshaticus*), to blue (*P. platypus*), to brown or gold (*L. aequispinus*), and as indicated, each are different species. It is indeed king-sized, growing to a healthy six feet from tip to tip, but one could say it's light on its toes as it usually weighs about six pounds. That is, of course, if not caught before then. Living on sandy or muddy shallows in Arctic

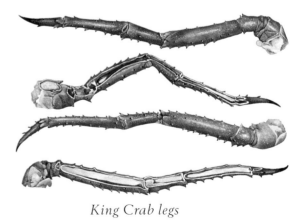

King Crab legs

waters, king crabs have been observed marching in herds across vast stretches of flat bottom. A strange and spectacular sight, for sure. For survival, juvenile king crabs depend on rocky, coarse structured habitat for protection in their first couple of years. Unlike its crab brethren, a king crab has only three pairs of walking legs, and two powerful claws. The entire animal is covered with sharp spikes and spines. These crabs are found from the Gulf of Alaska, Bering Sea, and Aleutian Islands, to the Sea of Okhotsk and Kamchatka. Females carry their eggs for 11 months before they hatch.

Dungeness Crab

HOW THEY'RE CAUGHT: When the Chesapeake's oyster populations all but disappeared, blue crabs rose to fame as the bay's most valuable commercial fishery. Catches increased five-fold over the past half-century. Most are caught off the coast of Virginia and in Chesapeake Bay with traps, nets, and dredges. When the state of Virginia decided to hand out crabbing licenses, a frenzy ensued, with thousands of people who never fished crabs before scrambling to grab their piece of the pie. When the experts realized the fishing pressure would be too much for the poor crabs to bear, they imposed even tighter controls.

One will find youngsters and families gathered along not-so-sleepy docks around Long Island and elsewhere on the East Coast in search of the rising tide of blue crabs in summer. Inevitably, they're equipped to the hilt, with buckets for the catch, fishing line, and packs of chicken for crab bait. Yes, chicken. An odd exchange of this life for that life, but surprisingly effective. Sometimes bait isn't needed for night-time crabbing: with a dip net and flashlight, blue crabs can be shone upon and simply scooped up as they swim past at the water's surface. Screams of delight pierce the air as the scene transforms into a combination of pep-rally and countdown. Very thrilling indeed for young and old alike.

Fishing for dungeness in San Francisco Bay goes way back to 1848, though the fishery there today is very small. They're caught from Kodiak and southeast Alaska to central California with circular or square wire mesh crab pots that are submerged on the bottom, usually kept "soaking" overnight. These baited crab pots work by luring passing crabs into the cage from which only undersized crabs can escape. Crabbing here is managed by allowing only mature adult males to be kept during certain seasons (females and small males are thrown back). The states manage fishing for this species and enforce consistent rules in both state and federal waters.

Red king crabs are taken with huge square, wire-mesh traps. The 1960s and 1970s seemed to be a high-point for red king crabs in the Aleutians, as they've never been so abundant as they were then. The catch is managed by the state of Alaska under a federal plan that includes limited access, closed areas, size limits, seasons, permit requirements, and numerous other measures. Federal observers are even put on board these crab vessels to monitor compliance with regulations.

The North Pacific Fishery Management Council and the State of Alaska tailor their regulations according to how the three distinct populations of Tanner crabs are doing. Hence, Bering Sea Tanner crabbing can be halted while the others continue.

In one of the sadder stories, fishing is no longer allowed for snow crabs in much of their former range because of revelations about how poorly they're doing and higher management standards.

Fishers use traps called pots to catch stone crabs. But get this: Only the larger claw is taken, with the animal returned to sea alive. They live to grow a new claw in 18 months. Florida brings in the most stone crabs of any state.

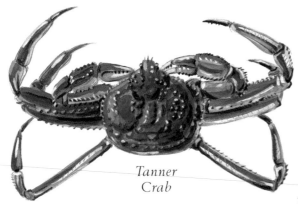

Tanner Crab

Tanner crabs live in the North Pacific and Bering Sea, from Oregon to Kamchatka. Living about six years, and the males grow to be about a third larger than their females counterparts. An interesting phenomenon with female Tanner crabs when they're ready to mate is the creepy-crawly mounds they form of about 100 or so crabs. Scientists think these mating aggregations, known as "pods," could be a means of protection from predators, or it could be a way to attract males. Female Tanners lay 50,000 to 400,000 eggs at a time, and they can retain live sperm for up to two years.

Snow crabs are bi-coastal. In the Pacific, they occupy the continental shelf of the Bering and Chukchi seas, and are believed to extend into Russian waters, but it's not known how far. In the western Atlantic they occur from the Canadian maritimes south to Maine. Mature females rarely grow much larger than three inches (males four), and cease to grow after their last molt. These crabs eat shellfish, brittle stars, other crabs, worms, and small fish they find on the bottom. In turn, they are eaten by cod, halibut, eel pouts, sculpins, skates, and bearded seals.

Stone Crab claws

**NUTRITION:
BLUE CRAB**

100 calories
10 fat calories
1 g total fat
90 mg cholesterol
20 g protein
8% calcium
4% iron

(Based on a 3 oz. serving size. Vitamins and minerals are based on 2,000 calorie diet.)

Stone crabs live in nearshore waters such as bays, estuaries, and tidal creeks from Texas to North Carolina. They're very similar to dungeness crabs in their shell attire, with their black-tipped big claws, one bigger than the other, looking as though they just emerged from an inkwell. Perhaps a crab version of a manicure! Their reddish shell gets to be about five inches across and they can weigh up to a hefty pound and a half.

Jonah crabs live offshore around rocky areas in deep water of the Atlantic from Maine and New Hampshire north to Prince Edward Island.

How They're Doing: Recent surveys indicate a significant, long-term decline in these beautiful swimmers in Chesapeake Bay waters, where they suffer from the one-two punch of overfishing and habitat destruction. They're doing better, however, in other parts of their range. Dungeness crabs are presently abundant off California, Oregon, Washington, and Alaska. After a huge peak in the late 1970s, the red king crab population collapsed. The num-

Do shellfish contain a lot of cholesterol? NO.

Shellfish were at one time believed to be high in cholesterol, but new measuring techniques indicate that cholesterol levels of most shellfish species are much lower than previously thought. Shellfish contain very little saturated fat, which is what causes our bodies to manufacture cholesterol. Cholesterol levels in such crustaceans as crab and lobster are similar to that found in the dark meat of chicken. While cholesterol in shrimp varies considerably by species, it is generally almost two times higher than the dark meat of chicken, but far less than the cholesterol present in eggs. Here are some comparative cholesterol counts for shellfish, based on comparable serving sizes:

shrimp	165 mg
scallops	55 mg
oysters	115 mg
clams	55 mg
blue crab	90 mg
lobster	60 mg

ON EATING THEM

A lucrative market has recently developed for live king crabs.

Tanner and snow crabs are nearly indistinguishable except for their size: Tanners are larger.

The viscera of dungeness crab may contain heat-resistant biotoxins, and health officials recommend it not be eaten.

bers of small males and females steadily increased in a few areas. Fishing is prohibited in many places where king crabs used to be abundant. This, to give them a break and help them rebuild. No fishing has been allowed for Tanner crabs in the Bering Sea since 1996 because they became so depleted there. Snow crabs in the Bering Sea don't appear to be doing much better, and there are serious concerns that any blip by Nature or Human could send the population into a tailspin. No one knows for sure why they're doing so poorly. Stone crabs seem to be doing just fine.

Special Issues: The Chesapeake Bay is a sink for pollution and agricultural fertilizers from the slopes of six states. Not surprisingly, once-abundant eel grass is now a mere shadow of its former self, and blue crabs are following suit in part because they rely on these seagrasses and clean water to survive.

While there is significant bycatch of females and sub-legal males in Bering Sea crab fisheries, fishers return them to sea alive. There's an interesting setup in Alaska and the Bering Sea to minimize bycatch. If fishers fishing for groundfish catch crabs, those crabs are accounted for in the total crab fishery catch. This technique is uncommon in the world of fisheries management because in most cases bycatch is not considered in estimating how many of which animals are being removed from nature. Alaska managers elevate honesty to a new level with this policy. Not only do they keep track of by-caught crabs, they count them against the total allowed to be caught and will shut down the groundfish fishery for the season if too many crabs are being taken.

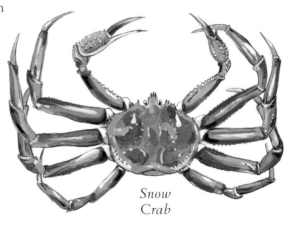

Snow Crab

Dungeness Crab Salad

SERVES 6

INGREDIENTS

½ lb. cooked crab meat (picked)

½ tsp curry powder

2 cups cooked peas

½ cup mayonnaise

2 cups cooked white rice

Crisp salad greens

Salt and pepper to taste

Gently combine all ingredients except salad greens in bowl.

Mix gently to combine.

Refrigerate, covered, 1 hour.

Serve on salad greens.

From the Gustavus Inn, Glacier Bay Alaska.
Contributed by the Lesh family, who have owned and operated the Inn for several generations.

Farmers' Charmers

Farmed Atlantic Salmon, Catfish, Crawfish, Rainbow Trout & Tilapia • Shrimp

Crawfish Étouffée
à la Ruth

SERVES 10

INGREDIENTS

¼ cup flour
¼ cup bacon grease
  (or cooking oil)
1 ½ cup chopped onions
1 cup chopped green
onions
1 cup chopped celery,
  with leaves
1 cup chopped bell pepper
2 cloves garlic, minced
  (or to taste)
1 four ounce can tomato
sauce
2 cups chicken bouillion
5 tsp salt (or to taste)
1 tsp pepper
½ tsp red pepper (option-
al)
Tobasco sauce to taste
1 tsp sugar
1 tsp Worcestershire sauce
1 TBSP lemon juice
1 bay leaf
½ cup chopped,
  fresh parsley
2-3 pounds crawfish tails
2-3 cups cooked rice

First, you make a roux: in a large heavy pot (traditionally cast iron), heat the flour and grease slowly, stirring constantly until it is dark brown (about the color of dark brown sugar—be careful not to let it burn).

Add onions, green onions, celery, bell pepper and garlic. Saute until soft(20-30 minutes).

Add tomato sauce, bouillion and the rest of the seasonings, except parsley.

Simmer slowly for about an hour, covered, stirring occasionally. (May need a bit of additional liquid—wine, beer, or water—but it should be a thick "gravy.")

Add crawfish and cook until done, 5-15 minutes.

Let it sit a while, if possible. This is really better if it's made the day before.

Reheat, but do not boil. Freezes well.

Add parsley just before serving over rice.

Ruth Guidry Ewell recipe compliments of Jerry Speir and Barbara Ewell, New Orleans.

*Brown Bullhead
Catfish*

Farmed Freshwater Fish

OVERALL RECOMMENDATION:

Farmed rainbow trout, catfish, tilapia, and crawfish rate a GREEN on the Fish Scale. Farmed Atlantic salmon rates a RED because of disease and habitat problems it causes for wild salmon. Some farmed fish can take pressure off depleted wild fish. Much of the fish-raising business has evolved to address many of its early-day problems, especially those using closed system technology (tanks). Catfish is a good substitute for orange roughy. Tilapia can substitute for grouper, as crawfish can for lobster. If tilapia are artificially raised in closed systems in the U. S., this fish is the closest thing there is to a vegetarian barn animal with gills.

Note: *See sections covering clams, shrimp, striped bass, and salmon for more on fish farming and a view of them in their wild states.*

From the "Farm": Channel catfish farming began in the 1960s in Arkansas, and subsequently spread elsewhere in the south. **Farmed catfish** tip in at 1.5 to five pounds, unlike their wild ancestors, whose record weight is 57 pounds! **Wild catfish** feed on muddy bottoms, their whiskers aiding in feeling around for food. But farmed catfish are fed pellets that float on the surface, eliminating the "muddy" flavor typical of their wild counterparts. Catfish are herbivores, with the pellets for farmed feed stamped out from soybeans, corn, wheat, and added vitamins and minerals.

A type of freshwater cichlid originating from the African continent, **tilapia** is now farmed all over the world. In the wild, some are "guarders," meaning they start out by brooding their eggs in nests, keeping the embryonic young clean of debris and well-oxygenated. Others are "mouth-brooders," wherein the fish pick up fertilized eggs from the nest they've built and keep them in their mouth until they're hatched. They come in a variety of colors from orange to green or white, and many sold are hybrids. The farmed varieties are brought to market at around one to two pounds.

Catfish: frozen whole, steaks and fillets; fresh as whole fish or fillets; nuggets, strips; breaded portions; smoked; minced; marinated
Tilapia: live fish market; fresh; frozen; whole; boneless fillets; marinated; breaded
Rainbow Trout: whole; filleted; smoked

Fish Scale

Farmed Rainbow Trout

Catfish

Crawfish

Tilapia

Maine Farmed Salmon

Farmed Atlantic Salmon

Tilapia

fish fact

Nearly half of the salmon sold in the U.S. are farmed.

It takes 2.8 pounds of other fish to grow every one pound of farmed salmon.

NUTRITION: CATFISH

170 calories
80 fat calories
total fat 9 g
55 mg cholesterol
21 g protein

(Based on a 3 oz. serving size. Vitamins and minerals are based on 2,000 calorie diet.)

RAINBOW TROUT

140 calories
50 fat calories
6 g total fat
60 mg cholesterol
21 g protein
6% calcium

(Based on a 3 oz. serving size. Vitamins and minerals are based on 2,000 calorie diet.)

All **rainbow trout** marketed in the U.S. is farmed, since selling the wild variety is strictly prohibited. More pink than "rainbow," farmers raise this species not only in the U.S. but throughout the world.

Farmed crawfish come from a huge family of more than 350 species worldwide. The Red Swamp crawfish is the main farmed species in the U.S., coming mainly from Louisiana. These freshwater crustaceans look like miniature lobsters, growing to about nine inches long.

How They're Doing: The fish farming business is booming. Farms provide a consistent supply of uniformly-sized animals, year-round—a predictability valued by many seafood purchasers, particularly the airline industry. The numbers of farmed fish are so controlled that it's useless to apply standard estimates of "abundance" as is done to define the health of wild populations.

Nearly half of the salmon sold in the U.S. are farmed. Commercially available Atlantic salmon in the U.S. are all farmed fish. The animals used to breed farmed Atlantic salmon come mostly from European rivers. Atlantic salmon are farmed in the maritimes, Maine, and Europe, sometimes to the detriment of the remaining runs of rapidly declining wild Atlantic salmon.

On Eating Them: Look for closed-system-grown aquaculture animals as ecologically less damaging. Farmed catfish ranks the fifth most consumed fish in the U.S. Many American-raised tilapia go for the live fish market, while fresh tilapia comes from Colombia and Costa Rica. The U.S. imports frozen versions of these fish from Indonesia, Taiwan, and Thailand. Other producers include Israel, Indonesia, Malaysia, Philippines, Mexico, Jamaica, and South America. Europe is another major principal consumer of tilapia. All farmed rainbow trout come from the U.S.

fish names

Atlantic Salmon
(S. salar)

Catfish *(I. punctatus)*

Crawfish *(P. clarkii):*
crayfish

Tilapia
(Oreochromis spp.)

Trout *(O. mykiss)*

Special Issues: It was once thought that if farmed Atlantic salmon escaped from their pens that they wouldn't fare well in the wild. However, farmed Atlantic salmon moved to farms on the Pacific coast turned out to be problematic for native salmon there. Atlantic salmon transplanted to the West Coast are escaping, competing with and threatening native salmon with diseases. The state of Washington has gone so far as to designate escaped Atlantic salmon a "pollutant" there because of anticipated effects on wild salmon.

At most outdoor aquaculture operations, fish-eating birds—like cormorants, terns, and herons—visiting for a ready feast are considered vermin, and shot. Some shooting occurs legally via permit, but there is much illegal shooting. Escaped tilapia or ones introduced into free flowing waters in tropical areas can have negative consequences for native fishes.

Crawfish

fish fact

The "whitefish" in smoked whitefish, whitefish salad and similar kosher dishes is a freshwater species related to salmon and trout. They are wild-caught in cold water Canadian and U.S. lakes and rivers with gillnets and traps usually through winter ice.

The fish in "gefilte fish" is carp, caught in lakes and rivers.

HOW THEY'RE FARMED: Catfish are raised in closed systems primarily in Arkansas, Mississippi, Alabama, and Louisiana. Tilapia are raised in the U.S., Colombia, Costa Rica, Indonesia, Taiwan, and Thailand. But not all tilapia and catfish come from closed-system aquaculture facilities. Unlike most farmed fish, which are fed large amounts of wild-caught fish, catfish and tilapia in the U.S. are generally fed an artificial, high-protein diet including much vegetable content such as soy protein and corn gluten. Interestingly, crawfish are often grown in rice fields, alternating seasons with this prized grain of the south.

Farming Ocean Life

The products of aquaculture in the United States have gained popularity over the last decade or so. The value of farm-raised seafood grew from about $500 million in 1989 to nearly $1 billion in 1998.

Hatchery Vs. Farm-Raised Fish. Farmed fish like Atlantic salmon are not deliberately released into the ocean. They are grown in pens and then sent to market (except for the inevitable escapees). Hatchery fish are grown to a certain size and then released into the wild. Hatchery-originated salmon on the West Coast are fin-clipped so that fishers can easily identify them from the depleted wild salmon that they must try to avoid catching. Today, a major proportion of salmon runs in the Pacific Northwest are from hatchery-raised fish. Some aquaculture facilities are constructed as closed systems which helps control pollution and escapees. Other facilities are open systems—ponds or net pens—containing the fish or shrimp in wetland areas or at river mouths. Closed systems generally cause fewer pollution, escape, introduced disease, predator-killing, and habitat problems than do open systems (ponds or pens).

Turning Fish Into Crops. Upon hearing about so many wild species on the decline, people frequently think that raising fish will help make up for the shortfall and give wild populations a break. Unfortunately, aquaculture has not reduced the pressure on wild populations. Strangely, it may do the opposite. A major reason is the world's rapidly growing human population, creating an ultimately unsustainable demand for food and nutrition. More than twice the amount of seafood (fresh and salt water) comes from aquaculture compared to ten years ago. Overall, aquaculture supplies one-fifth of the fish people eat worldwide.

Overfishing. One reason aquaculture ultimately can't be our ocean savior is because most fish need to eat other fish for food. We still have to go fishing to feed the fish that are farmed. And catching fish to feed the fish that are farmed means there are fewer fish in the wild to serve as prey for the fish that are wild. In some countries, shrimp farmers invest in trawl nets with fine mesh to catch everything they can for shrimp food, a practice known as

Pros:
- Supplies seafood—may offset some decline in capture fisheries
- Provides some jobs in coastal areas
- Rejuvenates seafood processing industry in some areas
- Limited enhancement of wild populations in some cases

Cons:
- Additives in seafood:
  - antibiotics
  - hormones
- Water pollution:
  - excessive nutrients from waste products
  - pesticides
- Accidental escape effects on wild populations of native species
- Release of exotic species
- Genetic dilution of wild species
- Genetically engineered or hybrid organisms
- Introduction and spread of disease
- Property rights and user conflicts in coastal and offshore areas
- Intensive water requirements
- Potential for displacement of subsistence fishers in wild capture fisheries
- Habitat loss for natural populations of wildlife
- Wildlife conflicts, especially efforts to reduce predators (i.e. shooting seabirds or marine mammals that feed on penned fish)

"biomass fishing." Aquaculture also threatens marine fish because some of its most valuable species, such as groupers, milkfish, and eels, cannot be bred in captivity and are instead raised from newly hatched fish caught in the wild: the constant loss of young fry can lead these species even further into decline.

Habitat Loss. Aquaculture is a source of disease and pollution, and a leading cause of coastal habitat destruction in some regions, undermining the survivability of wild juvenile fishes dependent on these near-shore nursery habitats to feed and grow. Fish farms can hurt wild populations because the construction of pens along the coast often requires destroying wetlands or cutting down mangroves—the submerged roots of these salt-tolerant trees provide a natural nursery for wild shrimp and fish.

Exported Riches. Aquaculture proves a poor replacement for fishing jobs because it requires substantial investment, land ownership, and large amounts of clean water. Most of the people living on the crowded coasts of the world lack all these resources. Aquaculture, as carried out in many undeveloped nations, often produces only shrimp and expensive types of fish for export to richer countries like the U.S., leaving most of the locals to struggle for their own needs with the oceans' declining resources.

A combination of record catches of wild and hatchery-raised fish, and millions more produced on salmon farms in Chile, Great Britain, and Scandinavian countries has glutted world salmon markets. As a result, prices paid to fishers have plummeted. Many are going bankrupt and some canneries are closing.

Technology Improving. Fish and shrimp farming can be done with less damage. In some places, aquaculture facilities are sited on land, minimizing ecological impact and making it more feasible to treat waste water and prevent escapes and the spread of diseases. Tilapia and catfish have been successfully farmed in closed systems. So have some shrimps and hybrid striped bass. Some Atlantic salmon farmers in Maine rotate their fish-raising pens to give these areas time to recover. This proves to be effective in reducing disease, pollution, and predation problems.

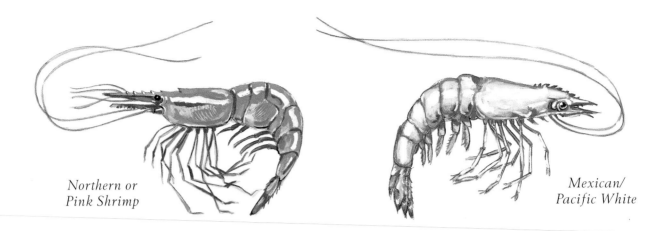

Northern or Pink Shrimp

Mexican/ Pacific White

Shrimp

Fish Scale

California trap-caught Spot Prawns

Atlantic Northern Pink Shrimp

In the Wild: Shrimp in myriad varieties can be found in waters all over the world. Many are tiny and not used commercially. They grow fast and reproduce at a year or two. Some types of shrimp dig and share their burrows with gobies, a small fish. They do this because they have poor eyesight and the gobies give their landlord shrimp the heads up when potential predators come near. Some shrimps change sex in order to reproduce; some clean parasites off big fish. Overall, shrimps are highly prolific breeders, living short lives, reproducing quickly, and spawning many eggs.

Pink shrimp occupy mud, sand or clay bottoms in waters from 50 to nearly 5,000 feet deep off the North American Pacific and Atlantic coasts. They are naturally pink, and change from males to females when they are a year and a half old. After spawning in September and October, peak hatching occurs during late March and early April.

Pacific white shrimp grow to seven inches, occupying warm to cool waters from 300 to 600 feet deep. This group includes Chinese white shrimp and fleshy prawn. Also cultured in China, white shrimp took a serious hit when 70 percent of pond (farmed) populations died from disease.

OVERALL RECOMMENDATION:

RED on the Fish Scale for most because catching wild shrimp entails serious bottom habitat destruction and high by-kill. Most shrimp farms destroy natural habitat and create pollution or disease problems. Atlantic northern pink shrimp fall in the GREEN because they're abundant and bycatch is not a problem, but it's mostly exported and not widely available for consumers in North America. California trap-caught spot prawns are the best choice and rate a GREEN on the Fish Scale. However, be aware that half the spot prawns brought to market are trawl-caught, which we place in the RED zone due to by-kill and habitat concerns.

Trawl-caught Spot Prawn

Most Shrimp

Shrimp: whole cooked, cooked and peeled, canned, frozen, frozen raw, headless, frozen peeled and de-veined, breaded, butterflied, and even live (Pacific White)

Gulf Pink Shrimp

Shrimp are consumers' #1 seafood item. No surprise that they are the most lucrative, top-value species for seafood producers. Yet, the pursuit of this beloved crustacean is one of the biggest bad news stories in fishing. Four to 10 pounds of unwanted marine life are discarded worldwide for every pound of shrimp kept.

Black tiger shrimp are easy to recognize because of the gray-black stripes on their thick shell. These grow to monster-size—13 inches—on mud bottoms from shallow water to 300 feet deep.

Gulf pink shrimp have a red to light brown shell. It's the largest of the Gulf shrimp (11 inches) and live on mud and silt bottoms from the Atlantic through the Gulf of Mexico.

Gulf brown and **white shrimp** can be difficult to distinguish. Brown shrimp females grow to about eight inches long. Gulf whites are more translucent than Gulf browns, with blue and green on their legs and tail. Both species inhabit mud, peat, sand, or clay bottoms.

Because they're fast-growing and mature early (120 days), shrimp farmers favor **Pacific white** for farming, particularly in Mexico, and Central and South America. They are similar in size and appearance to Gulf white shrimp. *P. vannamei* occur naturally from Sonora, Mexico, to northern Peru in mud bottoms, while *P. Stylirostris* is found from Baja California to Peru in mud, sand or clay bottoms.

Chinese White

Another hermaphrodite, **California spot prawns** change from male to female at about two years old right as they prepare to spawn. Really a shrimp, not a prawn, spot prawns are so called for their four bright white spots. (Ridgebacks, also found in California, are called shrimp but really are prawns).

NUTRITION: SHRIMP

80 calories
10 fat calories
total fat 1 g
165 mg cholesterol
18 g protein
No carbohydrates,
  sugars or fiber
More than 2 percent
  iron and calcium

(Based on a 3 oz. serving size. Vitamins and minerals are based on 2,000 calorie diet.)

How They're Doing: How they're doing is a mixed-bag: they're depleted in some regions while plentiful in others (see accompanying table). There's high by-kill in the way most are caught (see Special Issues below). The exceptions are Atlantic northern pink and California spot prawn.

Special Issues: In the southern U.S., as much as four pounds of unwanted creatures are killed for every pound of shrimp caught. This by-kill contributed over the last 20 years to an 85 percent decline in the Gulf of Mexico population of reef fishes like snappers and groupers—

FARMED SHRIMP FOOD

The food fed to farmed shrimp contains 33 percent fish oil and fish meal—made from wild-caught anchovies, herrings, menhaden, and sardines, and from by-kill of other fish (often from shrimp trawls). Other components of shrimp food are wheat, soybean meal, and other fillers. Twenty-five percent of all the shrimp consumed in world markets is farmed.

It's estimated that world trade in shrimp is US$8.5-9 billion per year.

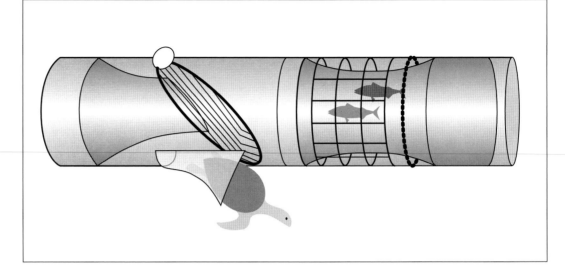

Shrimp trawl *turtle excluder and bycatch reduction devices. Gear modifications like these help fish and turtles escape, reducing harmful bycatch. From this perspective, the shrimp boat would be towing the device to the left. The shrimp net itself would be a small-meshed elongated sack attached at the right end of the tube.*

HOW THEY'RE CAUGHT: Shrimp fishers all over the world use bottom trawls, severely disrupting habitats. With a few exceptions, fishing for shrimp takes place year-round. Although the fishing vessels used vary in size and technology, the practice is pretty much the same. For all shrimp fishing, by-kill ranks the worst of any fishery in the world: from four to 10 pounds of creatures are discarded worldwide for every pound of shrimp kept. The rare exception is a trap fishery for spot prawns off the U.S. West Coast.

In the U.S., regulators use a variety of management tools to curtail the problems inherent with shrimp fishing, including setting by-kill limits, prohibiting fishing for them during spawning in certain areas, restricting gear (including mandating specific equipment to reduce by-kill—see below). In the Gulf of Mexico, the number of boats and the amount of fishing done for shrimp is more than the shrimp can take. Elsewhere in the world, management is inadequate or non-existent.

Some shrimp fisheries must use technological devices to reduce by-kill to discarded by-kill. For example, most U.S. shrimp fisheries are required to use trap-door devices to allow sea turtles to escape the net. But even in these fisheries, the nets still drag bottom, which harms habitat, and many turtle-safe shrimp fishing operations still kill lots of juvenile fish.

The amount of shrimp from farming has increasingly replaced trawl-caught shrimp in many areas of the world, particularly southeast Asia, the Indo-Pacific, and China. In the 1980s and '90s, aquaculture boomed, stimulated by the popularity and high cash value of shrimp. By 1994, pond-farmed shrimp produced five times the amount of shrimp than had been cultivated a mere decade previously. The intense growth of shrimp farming takes its toll on coastal mangrove habitat, local water quality, and regional supplies of fish, much of which went into feed for rearing shrimp. Hasty development was not without its costs to the industry, as overcrowding, overfeeding, and poor water use led to disease outbreaks that swept through the farms, and continue to be serious problems. (See "Aquaculture Pros and Cons," page 61.)

*Black Tiger
Shrimp*

fish fact

PRAWN VS. SHRIMP

Large shrimp are often referred to as prawns. (California spot prawn is really a shrimp.) One true prawn is the freshwater species—*M. rosenbergii*—native to India, Pakistan, and southeast Asia in the wild—is widely cultivated just about everywhere and is the prawn you'll likely encounter in restaurants, especially swimming in live tanks.

which themselves support commercial fisheries. Some people who once fished for adult snappers in the Gulf have been forced to fish for other species or driven out of the fishing business altogether. By-kill of sea turtles in shrimp gear contributed to their decline off U.S. coastal waters and around the world. Now, shrimp in the western Gulf of Mexico and South Atlantic are caught using gear technology to reduce by-kill. The U.S. government can also require imported wild shrimp to be caught using specialized gear to reduce by-kill of sea turtles.

Disease outbreaks from introduced, non-native shrimps for farming purposes is common and pose a serious threat to native shrimp species in many places.

The power of the consumer in asking for high environmental standards is well-illustrated in the case of shrimp farming. In the 1990s, environmental groups began bringing to public attention the downside of shrimp aquaculture (see "Aquaculture Pros and Cons," page 61). Driven by economics and the fear of consumer boycotts, the shrimp aquaculture industry is developing standards and guidelines for its operations to address serious water pollution and disease problems. ("The industry" here is not one entity: it encompasses far-flung interests that are loosely coordinated by their central mission of making shrimp aquaculture successful.) The industry recognizes that addressing many of the issues that cause environmental problems (overfeeding, intensive use of antibiotics, poor siting and construction, etc.) can lead to more efficient and therefore more profitable shrimp farming. Shrimp that is farmed according to these standards has a lower impact on the environment. These standards are evolving and are not universally applied, but efforts are ongoing to clean up the industry and make it environmentally and socially safe and economically profitable. Until we get there, it counts to be vigilant about the shrimp you eat.

Markets: Half the shrimp sold are farmed. Demand for shrimp in Japan, the U.S., and Europe drives shrimp fishing and farming everywhere else in the world. Mexico, Guatemala, Ecuador, Indonesia, Australia, China, India, Thailand, Nicaragua, and Columbia all export shrimp. Even though China cultures shrimp, it has to import shrimp to meet high consumer demand.

Know Your Shrimp

Species	Features	Origins	Status
Pacific Northern Pink (*P. jordani*)	Change from males to females when 1.5 years old; pink in color	Unalaska in the Aleutian Islands to San Diego, California	High by-kill. Depleted off Alaska, but not overfished. Populations doing well off OR, WA, CA
Atlantic Northern Pink (*P. borealis*)	Very small with largest reaching 5 inches, pink in color	From northern Canada to Massachusetts; also off Greenland, Iceland, and northern Europe	New technology has reduced by-kill. Not overfished
White (*P. chinensis, and P. orientalis*)	Grow to 7 inches	Yellow Sea, East China Sea and Korean Bight	Cultured in China, causing habitat problems. Status unknown.
Black Tiger (*P. monodon*)	Gray-black stripes on thick shell; grow 13 inches long; one of the two most widely farmed shrimps	Native to eastern and southeast Africa, the Red Sea, and Arabian Gulf, around the Indian subcontinent and through-out Malaysia to Australia and Japan	High by-kill. Overfished and depleted in the wild. Highly farmed in Asia and the Philippines, causing habitat problems
Gulf Pink (*P. duorarum*)	Red to light-brown shell; 11 inches large	Atlantic coast and Gulf of Mexico	High by-kill. In the safe zone abundance-wise
Gulf Brown (*P. aztecus*)	Its whiskers are half again as long as its body	Massachusetts south through the Gulf of Mexico to Campeche	High by-kill. In the safe zone abundance-wise
Gulf White (*P. setiferus*)	More translucent than the brown	New Jersey to Florida and Gulf of Mexico	High by-kill. In the safe zone abundance-wise
Pacific White (*P. vannamei, P. chinensis, P. orientalis*)	Short-lived (120 days); *P. vannamei* is one of the two most widely farmed shrimps	From Sonora, Mexico to northern Peru	High by-kill. Wild-caught ones depleted in Gulf of California. Cultivated in Mexico, Central, and South America, causing habitat problems
Pacific White (*P. stylirostris*)	White shells with blue-green tinge	Baja California to Peru	High by-kill. Ones in the Gulf of California are depleted
California Spot Prawns (*P. platyceross*)	They change sex to reproduce; live six years; four bright white spots on body	Alaska to San Diego	Low by-kill because trap-caught. Abundant

Comrades in Armor

Clams • Mussels • Oysters • Scallops

Fish & Shellfish Farming Terms

AQUACULTURE: the controlled cultivation of freshwater or saltwater fish or shellfish covering a range of techniques using closed systems (such as tanks) or open systems (such as hatcheries, netted pens, or seeding). Some species are brought to non-native habitats to be grown. Aquaculture can involve hybridization and genetic manipulation of organisms to enhance certain characteristics. Aquaculture includes mariculture.

MARICULTURE: exploiting natural marine (salt water) habitats to cultivate marine organisms. This could include shrimp farming along the coasts, netted pens to grow tuna in offshore waters, or "seeding" shellfish (see below), among other techniques.

CULTURED SHELLFISH: shellfish that are taken from one place and grown in another, more controlled environment to enhance productivity. Culturing techniques include using various surfaces ranging from oak poles placed in mud, ropes or mesh tubes suspended from rafts. The term also includes "seeded" shellfish (see below).

SEEDING: when young-stage shellfish are taken from their naturally occurring wild areas and redistributed. This enhances shellfish production enabling increased catches. Typically, they're commercially dredged or raked (tonged) when they reach the desired size.

FISH OR SHELLFISH FARMING: a general term the same as "Aquaculture" above.

For a discussion of the pros and cons of aquaculture, see page 61.

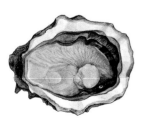

FARMED SHELLFISH: Shellfish like clams, oysters, and scallops do not require artificial food after their captive larval period. In this group, farmed animals are probably more ecologically benign than wild-caught ones, but there's plenty of room for argument. Shellfish also depend on the natural water filtration and food supply that come from coastal wetlands, so wetland loss directly damages shellfish habitat. Introduced farmed mollusks can also sometimes outcompete native species. Another drawback is that using non-native species in shellfish farming operations can spread diseases to native populations, sometimes with serious consequences. Nonetheless, wild and farmed shellfish require good, clean water, and many shellfish growers are active local advocates for clean water and healthy ecosystems. Worldwide, cultured shellfish comprises nearly half of all shellfish (excluding crustatceans) consumed.

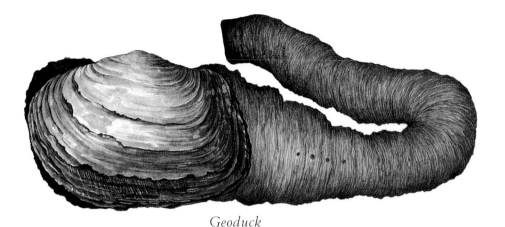

Geoduck

Clams

OVERALL RECOMMENDATION:

Wild clams can fall anywhere on the Fish Scale, depending on their local abundance and the method of catch. Clams—particularly hardshell clams, surf clams, and softshell clams—fall in the YELLOW zone of the Fish Scale because of by-kill and habitat problems with how they're captured. Ocean quahogs and geoducks fall in the RED zone of the Fish Scale because of their vulnerable life traits and the way they're caught damages habitat.

In the Wild: After starting out as free-floating larvae, clams clearly live a quiet, sedentary life. But when you look up close, you'll find there's more going on than meets the eye. They have a two-chambered siphon which serves multiple functions, from breathing, to catching food, to eliminating waste—a veritable snorkel of life. An army of cilia, or microscopic hairs, in the tube and gill chamber constantly move to keep the water circulating in and out. The rings evident on the outer shell are a good indication of how old a clam may be. Speaking of growth, new shell material is secreted at the edge of the clam via a thin layer of tissue called the "mantle" which covers the inside of the shell. Severe storms that drastically lower salinity or bring waves that pound exposed beaches have been known to destroy local clam populations. Defying their protective armor, a wide variety of creatures prey upon clams including fish, birds, marine mammals, crabs, ducks, worms, snails, starfish, rays, whelks, and of course, you and me.

The **hardshell clam**, also known as the bay Quahog, is a grayish brown to blue-black clam with a thick, symmetrical shell. It occurs in bays from Canada to the Gulf of Mexico. It can grow bigger than three inches, and is called by different names depending on the size and use of the meat, from smallest to largest: littlenecks, cherrystones, topnecks, and chowder clams.

Farmed
Clams

Hardshell
Surf, Softshell
Clams

Dredged
Clams

Ocean
Quahogs

Geoducks

Clams: sold live, fresh or frozen whole, shucked whole meats, minced, or chopped; processed for juice, canned, smoked, or as breaded clam strips.
Surf Clam shells used for "stuffed" seafood products.

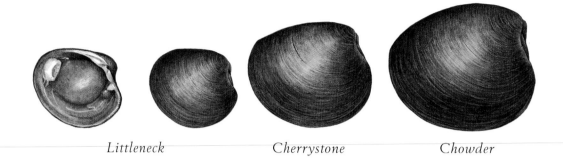

Littleneck   *Cherrystone*   *Chowder*

ON EATING THEM

Most clams available in U.S. markets are wild-caught. As filter feeders, clams accumulate pollutants from the water or organisms on which they feed. The waters and beaches from which clams are taken are certified for water quality as a protection against both pollutants and natural toxins that develop from red algae or "red tides." These can accumulate in shellfish flesh and poison unwitting diners if eaten raw. Knowing the source of your clams is important.

The **surf clam** is whitish brown, covered with smooth, concentric rings and fine hair. They are found from the southern Gulf of St. Lawrence to Cape Hatteras. In the mid-Atlantic region surf clams are found in commercial quantities from the beach to about 195 feet. They can grow to more than eight inches, but clams that size are unusual. They grow fast and mature young, reproducing in their first or second year.

The **softshell clam** is little, thin, and brittle, known to us mostly as steamers, fryers, mud clams, or longneck clams. They have a protruding siphon, so unlike most hardshell clams, their shells do not close all the way. This clam is actually an alien (non-native) off the U.S. West Coast, where it was accidentally introduced from the Atlantic in the 1870s. They naturally range from eastern Canada to North Carolina, in shallow intertidal areas.

The **geoduck** (pronounced "gooey-duck") of the Pacific Coast is the largest of all the North American clams. They'll grow more than nine inches and weigh up to nine pounds if allowed, though they typically weigh three pounds when brought to market. It sports an obscenely elongated protruding siphon many times longer than its shell. Its reputation could be that of a circus spectacle, but knowing that it can live an entire century renders the geoduck, instead, respectable. Geoducks reside from southeast Alaska to the Pacific Northwest (but occur as far south as southern California), preferring sandy, muddy bottoms to about 600 feet. They're also farmed.

The **ocean quahog** (pronounced "ko-hog") has a dark brown or black covering on the shell. This medium-sized clam can live for an impressive 70 to 150 years. After reaching 20 years it grows very slowly. Ocean quahogs live in the Atlantic from Newfoundland to Cape Hatteras and off northern Europe. They live in water typically around 100-150 feet deep, but can be found as deep as 800 feet. Quahogs prefer cooler water, so the farther south they are, the more offshore they'll be.

**NUTRITION:
CLAMS**

100 calories
15 fat calories
1.5 g total fat
55 mg cholesterol
22 g protein
10% Vitamin A
6% calcium
60% iron

*(Based on a 3 oz. serving
size. Vitamins and
minerals are based on
2,000 calorie diet.)*

Softshell Clam

Surf Clam

How They're Doing:

The state of hardshell clams varies according to locale. In the northeast, like Narragansett Bay, they've declined. In the mid-Atlantic, hardshell clams remain stable. In the mid-Atlantic, oceanic surf clams remain low but stable after having collapsed in the 1970s from over-exploitation. Softshell clams around Maryland, Massachusetts, Rhode Island, New Jersey, and eastern Long Island are doing well. Softshell clams are doing less well in Maine and Maryland due to unusually hot summers and reproduction problems. Clams are beginning to benefit as ground-fish are from no fishing areas around Georges Bank off New England. When ocean quahogs declined in the mid-Atlantic region, clammers shifted to previously unexploited areas. When quahogs become depleted, it takes a long time for these slow-growing animals to recover.

Special Issues:

By-kill is significant when clams are taken with hydraulic dredges, a process that often entails serious bottom habitat destruction.

Markets:

Countries that export captured and cultured clams are the U.S., Canada, Great Britain, and France. Primary consumers of clams are northern Europe, Canada, and the U.S.

fish names

Geoduck *(P. geodosa)*

Hardshell Clams
(M. mercenaria in the North, and *M. campechiensis* in the south)*: bay Quahog, littlenecks, cherrystones, topnecks, and chowder clams (names depending on size)

Ocean Quahog
(A. islandica)

Surf Clam
(S. solidissima): skimmer, hen, sea, giant, or bar clam

Softshell Clam
(M. arenaria): steamers, fryers, mud clams, or longneck clams

HOW THEY'RE CAUGHT: Wild clams are taken with tongs, hand rakes, by divers, and with hydraulic suction dredges. The fisheries for surf clams and ocean quahogs off the Atlantic coast are highly regulated, with good reason. About half of all clams taken in the U.S. are surf clams that come from New Jersey and Virginia, making them the most important commercial clam species in the U.S. The state of Washington manages the commercial and recreational take of geoduck clams. When farmed, clams are often hatched indoors, then put into natural waterways (a process called "seeding"). Farm-raised clams are hand-raked, hoed, or dredged, depending on location.

SERVES 6

INGREDIENTS

Seafood:

48 farmed clams

For the Sauce:

6 large garlic cloves

2 cups tomatoes, peeled
    and crushed (fresh
    Italian plum tomatoes
    and whole peeled
    canned tomatoes)

7 TBSP good
    olive oil

1 tsp crushed hot
    red pepper flakes

3-4 TBSP shredded,
    fresh basil

For the Pasta:

1 ½ pounds
    capellini pasta

3 TBSP sea salt

Capellini All'Istriana
Capellini with seafood sauce

Preparing the clams: For easier opening, set the clams in the freezer for 20 minutes to relax the muscle that clamps the shells together. Holding the clam over bowl to catch its juices, set it in the palm of one hand, the hinge with its indentation toward you. Hold the clam knife in your other hand, its blade poised between the shells at the opposite end, and guided by the fingers of your other hand. With the clam secure in you hand, force the blade between the shells, then cut around under the top shell to release the muscle. Rotate the blade between the shells to force them open. Run the blade under the body of the clam to release and remove it. Strain juices into a bowl, chop the clams, place in a separate bowl, and reserve.

Preparing the tomato sauce: Peel and crush the garlic. If your tomatoes are fully ripe, the flavor of your sauce should need no help from the can. However, if it's to be mostly canned tomatoes, the inclusion of even a few imperfect fresh plum tomatoes gives the sauce an illusion of freshness. In any case, fresh tomatoes should be peeled, quartered lengthwise, then seeded; canned tomatoes also need seeding.

Set a heavy, 12-inch frying pan over moderate heat. Add 2 tablespoons of olive oil and brown the crushed garlic very lightly. Add the tomatoes and pepper flakes and let simmer for 20 minutes.

Preparing the seafood sauce: Pour 2 tablespoons of olive oil into another frying pan and set over moderately high heat. Stir in the clams and almost immediately pour in the clam juice, being careful not to include any sand from the bottom of the container. Raise the heat to high and shake the pan, until the liquid comes to a boil. Adjust seasoning. Pour in the tomato sauce and bring to a boil again, shaking the pan. Check seasoning again, pour 2 tablespoons raw virgin olive oil and stir in basil. Set aside.

Preparing the pasta: Heat three quarts of water in a stock pot and add salt. Time this so that the water is at full boil by the time the sauce is ready in the previous step. Then stir the capellini into the boiling water—it takes only about 2 minutes to cook. Drain the pasta while still stiff and toss immediately with half of the hot sauce and a tablespoon of raw virgin olive oil. Serve topped with the remaining sauce.

*Recipe contributed by Lidia Mattichio Bastianich,
owner of Felidia's restaurant located in New York City*

New Zealand Green Mussels

 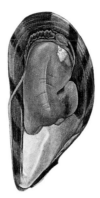

Blue Mussels

Mussels

Fish
Scale

Non-dredged
Cultured
Native
Mussels

Dredged
Mussels

OVERALL RECOMMENDATION:

Cultured (farmed) native mussels fall in the GREEN on the Fish Scale, but dredged mussels (whether seeded or wild) rank YELLOW because of the habitat damage caused in harvesting them. You can request to see the tag of origin that accompanies all shellfish from their beds to your point of purchase. So, check that they're native cultured mussels, and not dredged, and enjoy.

In the Wild: Dozens of varieties of these bivalve mollusks reside all over the world, only a couple of which are highlighted here. Mussels attach to a surface such as gravel, rocks, pilings (even on the legs of offshore oil platforms), and the like, by strong threads called "byssus threads." With a knob at the end of the threads, the animals move by attaching and pulling themselves forward by the threads, releasing and literally leaving these knots behind. But no illusions intended here, mussels don't move fast or go very far. Their inclination to attach themselves to something hard led to culturing techniques using various surfaces ranging from oak poles placed in mud, to ropes or mesh tubes suspended from rafts. Mussels have been cultured since the 13th century. Mussels can spawn almost continually if the conditions are just right. Severe storms can destroy local populations by heavy wave action or lowering salinity levels. As filter feeders, mussels are sensitive to water quality and are vulnerable to both human-caused and natural toxins. Their natural predators are many, including sea otters, seabirds, crabs, snails, starfish, fish, and on and on.

Blue mussels naturally reside in the Atlantic and Pacific. Their shells, elongated and narrow on one end, vary from blue-black to light brown with green streaks, with an iridescent inner shell. The blue mussel is cultured in Japan, Europe, Canada, the U.S., and reportedly also cultured in China.

fish names

New Zealand Green Mussels
(P. canaliculus)

Blue Mussels
(M. edulis):
Bay Mussels

Mediterranean Mussels
(M. galloprovincialis)

Mussels: live; frozen; smoked; and as meats: marinated or pickled

Mediterranean Mussels

ON EATING THEM

Mussel growing areas are sometimes closed as a result of "red tide," or plankton blooms. During times of heavy algal blooms, mussels can concentrate certain toxins that could be harmful to humans if eaten. Mussels are high in protein and vitamin A.

New Zealand green mussels are imported as seafood and not grown in U.S. waters. They're longer than blue mussels, with shells averaging four inches long, commonly growing eight inches or more. Their elongated shells are brownish green on one end, blending to green on the broad lip and marked with dark brown stripes. **Mediterranean mussels** are believed to be a race of U.S. native blue mussels.

How They're Doing:
Wild native blue mussel populations are stable in the Northeast U.S. Their status is unknown off the West Coast. Mediterranean mussels are farmed off the U.S. west coast.

Special Issues:
About half the mussels on U.S. markets are wild, and likely dredged, which damages bottom habitat. As filter feeders, mussels ingest microscopic plant and animal matter from the water. Shellfish beds from which mussels are taken are closely monitored for water quality.

Markets:
Mussels are taken from the wild in Canada, the U.S., Malaysia, South America, and the Caribbean. The U.S., Canada, New Zealand, France, Spain, Denmark, the Netherlands, and Italy grow and export cultured mussels.

HOW THEY'RE CAUGHT: Some truly wild mussel beds that are commercially exploited exist in Maine and Massachusetts. However, most commercially-targeted mussels from the wild have been "enhanced" by plucking some from shallow-water beds and redistributing the animals, which are then dredged, raked, or hand-plucked when they reach a desired size. These creatures are taken year-round, except during and just after spawning. Mussels are being increasingly farmed and cultured. Mediterranean mussels are grown in suspended systems (meaning the equipment and nets used to culture them are above the ground) in the Puget Sound, Washington. No commercial operations for truly wild—unenhanced, uncultured—mussels exist off the U.S. Pacific coast. New Zealand mussels are largely dredged.

American Oyster   *European Oyster*   *Japanese Pacific Oyster*

Oysters

Fish Scale

Japanese Pacific Oysters

European Oysters

Olympia Oysters

American Oysters

Dredged Oysters

OVERALL RECOMMENDATION:

This group rates a variety of colors on the Fish Scale, so ask questions if you want to indulge. American oyster is depleted and held back by water pollution, so it rates a YELLOW. While Olympia oysters are depleted, they're making a comeback. They're now well managed and have little habitat problems in the way they're harvested, so they fall in the GREEN zone. European oysters and Japanese Pacific oysters rate a GREEN on the Fish Scale. In this family of shellfish, farmed varieties can be environmentally problematic but are better than eating depleted species, especially if they are not dredged.

fish names

American Oyster
(*C. virginica*):
American blue point oyster

European Oyster
(*O. edulis*)

Japanese Pacific Oyster (*C. gigas*)

In the Wild: Oysters in myriad varieties inhabit nutrient-rich coastal ecosystems around the world. Oysters offered in markets originate from the wild or they're farmed. When farmed, they are often hatched indoors from wild spat (little baby oysters), then put into waterways to grow into adults. Because they filter nutrients through the water they imbibe, raising them depends on clean water, healthy habitats, and does not entail feeding except when first hatched.

How big oysters get and how they're shaped depends on the kind of bottom habitat they grow on. For example, rounder oysters tend to come from hard-bottomed habitats, and longer, more pointy oysters come from softer substrate. Upon close observation we can easily see how one oyster, not to mention an oyster colony, creates a microecosystem in itself. All manner of other shellfish, mud worms, barnacles, boring sponges, snails, hydroids, sea squirts, and numerous other creatures live among, on, and even inside oysters. A rise in water temperature come spring and summer triggers spawning that can be so prolific that it turns the water milky.

The eastern or **American oyster** resides from eastern Canada to the Gulf of Mexico. Its cupped, elongated, and irregular shell ranges from gray to brown with rose streaks. The American oyster populations all along the U.S. East Coast have fallen victim to water-borne

Oysters: live; shucked; fresh or frozen; smoked; canned

NUTRITION: OYSTER

100 calories
35 fat calories
3.5 g total fat
115 mg cholesterol
10 g protein
calcium 6%
iron 45%

(Based on a 3 oz. serving size. Vitamins and minerals are based on 2,000 calorie diet.)

diseases for many years. Oysters were the most valuable fishery in Chesapeake Bay for most of the 1900s, but overfishing and pollution knocked the species out of first place. A hundred years ago, it would take resident oysters merely a week to filter the entire volume of water in the Chesapeake Bay. Now it takes them more than a year because there are fewer oysters.

The most widely cultured oyster in the world, the **Pacific Japanese** oyster, comes originally from Japan. It's fast-growing and can get as big as 12 inches long, but it's usually taken when six inches or smaller. The rough, nubby shells vary from muddy brown to light gray. They can be found in shellfish farms sited in bays and coves and in the wild in many parts of the world. An introduced species that requires warm water to trigger spawning, the Japanese oyster spawns only erratically in U.S. West Coast estuaries. The Japanese Pacific oyster was first introduced to the West Coast to help boost British Columbia's declining commercial shellfish fishery, which had been based on the native Olympia oyster.

The only oyster native to the U.S. Pacific coast, the **Olympia oyster** takes five years to reach merely the size of a quarter. Because it's a slow-grower, it succumbs easily to overfishing. This green-shelled variety lives naturally from Baja California to Alaska in estuaries, small rivers and streams in either eel grass or mud flats. They are sensitive to extremes in temperature and pollution, and were nearly wiped out in the 1920s.

Shellfish farmers in Maine, New Hampshire, Washington, Oregon, and California almost exclusively culture the **European oyster** which is native to France. These oysters are rounder than American or Pacific oysters, with a flat upper shell that's brown or white. In four years they grow three to four inches, the size they're usually taken to market.

HOW THEY'RE CAUGHT: At one time, tongs and rakes were used to take oysters in the Chesapeake Bay, elsewhere along the Atlantic, and in waters fringing the Gulf of Mexico, but more destructive dredges replaced this method of removal. Oysters are captured year-round, except during months when they spawn. In the Chesapeake Bay, law requires oyster-dredging boats to be powered by sail, a restriction on technology that has helped this fishery survive. Since oysters occur near shore, their management is handled by state and sometimes local authorities. Conservation measures for wild oysters highly vary depending on the locale.

The materials used to suspend cultured oysters include fiberglass screens, grow-out trays, floats, suspended racks and sacks, rafts, and poles. Other oyster growers use either natural or hatchery-spawned spat to "seed" mud bottoms. Some oyster farmers specialize in native species, like the Olympia oyster which may be making a comeback in the Pacific northwest. Others prefer to farm the hardier, disease-resistant species like the Japanese oyster.

Comrades in Armor

ON EATING THEM

The way oysters taste depends on the waters in which they grow, even if they're the same species from one bay to another. There are a variety of naturally occurring toxins that are accumulated by oysters, even in water that is free from human pollutants. U.S. and Canadian waters where shellfish are taken are rigorously monitored and tested for toxins and contaminants. When shellfish waters are found to contain levels of contaminants unsafe for humans, a fishing advisory is issued for the affected areas, prohibiting collecting.

It's easy to tell the difference between the more benign net-grown and habitat-damaging dredged oysters: Net-grown Pacific Japanese oysters will have fluted shells. If they're seeded and dredged, they'll be smooth-shelled. Japanese oysters are the primary oysters consumed by Americans.

How They're Doing: In this group, farmed animals are in some ways more ecologically benign than wild-caught. Native oysters are vulnerable to overfishing, bad water quality, and competition from introduced, cultured species. Despite disease, pollution, hurricanes, and overfishing, native American oysters notably increased over the past few years in both the Chesapeake and Delaware bays, and Long Island. However, they remain overfished there and in the Gulf of Mexico. Olympia oysters are on the rebound but still seriously depleted. They've essentially been replaced in the market by the cultured alien Japanese Pacific oysters, the primary oyster consumed by Americans. Family-run farming operations are helping to bring back the Olympia oyster, which is considered a true delicacy for shellfish lovers particularly on the west coast where it is most available.

Special Issues: Dredging often entails serious bottom habitat destruction. Tonging and raking are less destructive but still somewhat disruptive to bottom habitat. Although growing oysters in suspended net systems avoids this problem, introductions of alien mollusks have spread diseases to native populations, with serious consequences. Because they are filter feeders and sensitive to water quality, oysters, whether native or wild, suffer from pollution and harmful algal blooms. The shellfish growing business depends on clean, natural waters.

Are oysters are an aphrodisiac? HMMmmm...

Well, we can't vouch for the truth of that claim, but here's what you should know about oysters and your health. If you have liver disease, diabetes, HIV or AIDS, or have used steroids for a long time, health specialists say you should not eat raw oysters. A naturally occurring bacterium, Vibrio vulnificus, is commonly found in Gulf of Mexico oysters. It occurs naturally in the marine environment, not from human pollution. Cooking completely kills the bacteria.

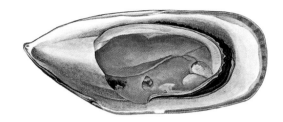

SERVES 6

INGREDIENTS

3 fire-roasted red and/or
yellow or orange bell
peppers
1 large red onion
2 TBSP butter

2 pounds Pacific Coast farm
raised clams, scrubbed
clean, in the shell
2 pounds Pacific Coast farm
raised mussels, scrubbed
and de-bearded
2 pounds Pacific Coast farm
raised small oysters
(Pacific yearlings,
Kumamotos, or Olympias)

2 cups water
1 TBSP olive oil
1 TBSP fresh jalapeno,
seeded and minced
5 large cloves garlic, minced
½ tsp salt
½ tsp black pepper
¼ tsp white pepper
¼ tsp allspice

4 cups fresh tomatoes,
peeled and chopped
2 TBSP fresh ginger, peeled
and minced
1 TBSP orange zest (rind),
grated
¼ cup scallions, finely
chopped (reserve 1 TBSP
for garnish)
¼ cup fresh cilantro,
minced (reserve 1 TBSP
for garnish)
3 cups clam juice
¾ cup tomato paste
1 ½ cups coconut milk
¼ pound shredded
(preferably unsweetened)
coconut

Brazilian Bouillabaisse

Over open flame, fire-roast or broil bell peppers, then peel, seed and slice thinly. Set aside.

Thinly slice onion, and sauté in pan with melted butter until carmelized (nicely browned). Set aside.

Sauté coconut in ungreased sauté pan, just until browned. Set aside.

Bring water to boil in large pot. Drop in clams, mussels, and oysters and cook for about 5 minutes, or until shells open. Remove from pan and refrigerate. Strain cooking liquid through sieve until liquid runs clear.

Reserve, refrigerated.

In large soup pot, heat olive oil over medium heat. Add prepared peppers and onion, jalapeño, garlic, peppers, and allspice. Sauté for 5 minutes. Add tomato, ginger, orange rind, scallions, cilantro (remember to reserve 1 TBSP scallions and cilantro for garnish), reserved shellfish broth, and additional clam juice to equal 3 cups. Add tomato paste. Cook over low heat, stirring occasionally, for about 30 minutes.

Add coconut milk and reserved shellfish and continue stirring over low heat for another 5 minutes or until almost reaching a boil.

Ladle into individual bowls. Garnish with browned coconut, reserved fresh cilantro, and reserved green onions.

Recipe courtesy of Robin Downey,
Pacific Coast Shellfish Growers Association.

Bay Scallop

Scallops

OVERALL RECOMMENDATION:

Scallops, no matter what species, rank RED on the Fish Scale if they're wild-caught because most of those sold in the U.S. are over-fished and they're taken with heavy metal dredges, causing serious bottom-habitat damage. If you know your scallops are native and farm-raised, then they fall in the GREEN zone because these production methods avoid overfishing problems, and have minimal pollu-tion problems. Japanese scallops–imported into the U.S. as seafood–are in the RED zone of the Fish Scale because they are dredged. Ask your seafood seller for suspension cul-tured scallops.

In the Wild: The world harbors more than 400 species of scallops. Unlike clams, mussels and oysters, which stay put once they settle to the bottom, scallops swim and move about quite adeptly when the need arises. They have a strong muscle that keeps the shell halves together, which they use to swim by clicking their shells together and pro-pelling backward. Like some other mollusks, scallops possess eyes (see illustration, next page) and chemoreceptors with which to sense their surroundings and potential predators.

Scallops born in muddy estuaries and bays are intimately dependent on healthy eelgrass beds, as the young scallops cling to leafy stems to keep from falling to the mucky bottom and suffocating. Bay scallops all but disappeared in the late 1920s and early thirties when eelgrass fell victim to a virulent fungus. But when eelgrass came back, so did the scallops. This episode underscores how diseases and depletions can occur naturally and that certain species have a natural, inherent capacity to rebound.

Come springtime when water temperatures increase, some scallops spawn numerous times over the course of several weeks. Like other filter feeders, they are vulnerable to pollution or natural toxins that affect water quality. Scallops prefer salty water without much freshwater flow, and can be found on hard bottoms, in salt ponds, coves, brackish bays, and on out to deeper water. Just about everybody likes scallops: creatures that prey on them include crabs, snails, starfish, finfish, and waterfowl.

The scallop most familiar to shellfish lovers is the **Atlantic sea scallop**, a native along the Atlantic coast off eastern Canada to North Carolina. It's fan-shaped, brownish, and grows to

Atlantic Sea Scallop
(P. magellanicus)

Bay Scallop *(A. irradians)*:
Cape Cod, Long Island
Peconic, or blue-eyed
scallop

Calico Scallop *(A. gibbus)*:
Cape scallop

Queen Scallop
(C. opercularis)

Icelandic Scallop
(C. islandica)

Pacific Sea Scallop
(P. caurinus)

Pink Scallop
(C. Rubida): singing, swimming, Hind's, or pecten
scallop

**Spiny or "Singing"
Scallops** *(C. hastata)*: Not
to be confused with the
pink scallop, also called the
singing scallop

Chinese Scallop
(C. farreri)

Japanese Scallop
(P. yessoensis)

*Scallops
possess
eyes*

fish fact

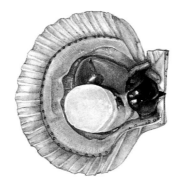

Queen Scallop

a full nine inches. Sea scallops generally scatter on the bottom near shore, but concentrations do exist in cooler, deeper water down to 600 feet. These scallops grow quickly and mature at around age two. However, they gain most of their size and weight when they're between three and five years old. They're commercially valuable at younger ages, before they have much chance to reproduce.

Unlike other scallops, the **bay scallop** spawns only once in its two-year life span. It lives in shallow inlets and bays mostly from Cape Cod to Long Island, but can be found as far south as North Carolina. It's also farmed in Nova Scotia, New England, South America, and China. The four-inch shells range from brown to purple, tan or orange.

The **calico scallop**, so-called for its speckled brown and white shell, is a tiny one, taken mostly when three inches or smaller. They occur in warm waters of the Gulf Coast, and around Central and South America. It's also called Cape scallop for that part of its home territory near Cape Canaveral, Florida.

One would imagine **queen scallops** to be as big and colorful as royalty would demand, but they're in fact small, with muted brown shells. They occur from Norway to the Canary Islands and in the western Mediterranean.

Icelandic scallops are about the same size as queen scallops, but with brownish green shells. **Chinese scallops** are similar to the Icelandic variety, and for commerce are entirely farmed.

The **Pacific sea scallop** ranges from Alaska to Oregon and is similar in size to the Atlantic variety.

Singing scallops, with pink and white shells, occur in Puget Sound, Washington, and grow to about three inches. They're often confused with pink scallops because of their similar size and coloration. Why they're called "singing" scallops is a mystery because they don't sing. At least not to their biggest predator: us.

Japanese scallops occur in the wild in Japan. They're fast-growing, reaching four inches within a year.

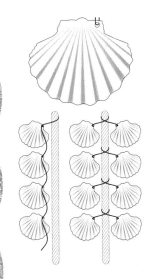

How They're Doing: Atlantic sea scallops are overfished off New England and the Mid-Atlantic. They're more abundant off New England in certain fishing-free zones because they benefited from closures instituted to protect groundfish, but this could change (see "How They're Caught"). See accompanying table for status and distribution information.

Special Issues: Scallop dredges anywhere and everywhere are very hard on bottom habitat, and bottom trawls modified for scallops aren't much better.

On Eating Them: Both fresh and frozen scallops are available year-round, although fresh ones are limited in the winter months. Beware of products offered as "bay scallops"—they may be queen scallops and large calico scallops. The best advice is to get to know your restaurateur or fish seller so you can be sure of their source. The availability of the more benign farm-raised scallops (whether from U.S. waters or imported) is miniscule compared to dredged scallops.

Markets: Imported farmed scallop meats from China compete with and have surpassed North American farmed scallops. Most scallops are shucked at sea, but processed ashore and marketed fresh. The U.S., Japan, China, and Canada all export cultured scallops. The U.S. imports wild-captured scallops from Mexico, Canada, Central America, Peru, Chile, Brazil, Philippines, Thailand, and China. Primary consumers are Japan, U.S., Spain and France.

NUTRITION: SCALLOPS

120 calories
10 fat calories
total fat 1.0 g
55 mg cholesterol
22 g protein

(Based on a 3 oz. serving size. Vitamins and minerals are based on 2,000 calorie diet.)

Ear-hanging Method for Cultivating Scallops:

Because netting and materials are becoming increasingly expensive, many culturists are turning to the more labor-intensive ear-hanging method. A small hole is drilled into the right ear of the shell. (One person can drill only 1500 holes a day.) Wire or monofilament line is used to secure scallops to suspended line. The lines are attached to floating rafts or individual floats. Ninety percent of scallops survive using this method. (Source: Washington State Department of Natural Resources.)

HOW THEY'RE CAUGHT: Wild-caught scallops (Atlantic sea, bay, calico, queen, Icelandic, and Pacific) are commercially taken from the bottom using dredges that destroy bottom habitat. The gear used is industrial in size and capacity, where heavy chains, spikes, and rollers scrape and churn up the ocean bottom to stir up the scallops. Managers in certain areas restrict scalloping via the number of fishing days allowed, closing off areas, and dictating the types of gear that can be used. In a highly controversial move, managers now allow scallop dredging in areas that are still closed to groundfish fishing, despite concerns that by-kill of young flounder in scallop dredges would impede flounder recovery. Notably, in some local, small-scale operations, wild scallops are caught with low-tech methods using rakes or tongs, or hand-picking by divers.

Some farm-raised scallops (Atlantic sea, bay, pink, and spiny) are cultured and grown on ropes or suspended nets which avoids the habitat-destructive problems associated with dredging. Many species are also "seeded," whereby farmers take newly-hatched larval-stage scallops from the wild (either native or alien species) and spread them around over a larger area, which has the effect of enhancing survival and increasing harvests. But they're taken with habitat-destructive dredges and rakes.

Know Your Scallops

Species	Wild Status	Wild: How taken & Where	Cultured: Farming Techniques Used & Where
Atlantic Sea Scallop	Overfished and depleted off New England and the Mid-Atlantic	● Dredges and otter trawls year-round from inshore waters from Virginia to Massachussets	● Newfoundland suspended nets in coastal waters, but rarely available in the U.S.
Bay Scallop	Overfished and depleted, but increasing in parts of their range; stable off Massachussets	● Tongs, dredges, rakes in shallow water from fall to early winter	● Suspended net systems in New England, Nova Scotia, South America, and China, but rarely available in the U.S.
Calico Scallop	Status unknown, but catches have been declining since the mid 1980s despite increasing fishing effort	● Trawled year-round in Florida and Gulf of Mexico from hard sand or mud bottom using modified shrimp gear, causing significant habitat destruction	
Queen Scallop	Abundant	● Dredged from Norway to the Canary Islands and in the western Mediterranean	● Seeded in wild waters and also via ● net suspension, depending on operation and locale. The latter is rarely available in the U.S.
Icelandic Scallop	Status unknown	● Dredged off Iceland, Faroe Islands, Norway, and Canada	
Pacific Sea Scallop	Status unknown	● Dredged in coastal waters from Alaska to Oregon	
Pink Scallop	Abundant; available only locally	● Hand-plucked by divers from Washington's Puget Sound	
Japanese Scallop	Wild status unknown	● Dredged in the wild	● Seeded in wild waters and then dredged

● Red on Fish Scale
● Green on Fish Scale

Restless Rascals

Anchovy, Herring, Sardine • Bluefish • Hake • Bass • Squid • Mackerel

Herring

Anchovy, Herring & Sardines

Fish
Scale

Herrings
Sardines
Anchovies

In the Wild: Herrings, sardines, and anchovies of many species (only a few of which are sold commercially and discussed here) are small fish that flit through the water in perfectly synchronized silvery schools. Schooling helps protect against predators. It's also thought that this behavior helps coordinate reproductive cycles, as they spawn in large gatherings. They occur in shallow waters throughout the world, except at the two poles. All of them strain small marine organisms from the water for food. This may be why they inhabit mostly shallow waters, as coastal areas are the most nutrient rich zone of all aquatic habitats.

Herrings are continuous schoolers. They also lack spines. Pacific herring can grow to 18 inches. These can be found in large schools near the surface from Korea to Japan to Alaska to northern Baja California. Herring swim against the currents to spawn in bays and estuaries, enabling the young to be easily carried back to feeding grounds. There are several separate breeding populations and some live longer and grow larger and faster than others. Herring near the coast off Alaska and California spawn in kelp beds and eelgrass. In addition to krill, zoo-plankton, copopods, and amphepods, herring eat small fish. They are in turn eaten by salmon, Pacific cod, dogfish, lingcod, seals, sea lions, porpoises, and seabirds, among others.

Atlantic herring are blue-green on the back, light on the belly, and average about a foot long. They occur off our coasts from Greenland to North Carolina, and in the eastern Atlantic.

OVERALL RECOMMENDATION:

The next time you cruise a smorgasbord, try the pickled herring. All these small pelagics earn a GREEN rating on our Fish Scale, but you may not even know that you're eating them because they're mainly processed into fish meal and oil used in other products.

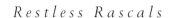

Anchovy: canned; fish oil for human consumption; fish meal and oil for fertilizer and animal feed
Herring: fresh and frozen; whole or filleted; pickled; salted; canned; smoked; roe valuable
Sardines: mostly caught for bait and fish meal, but some are also sold fresh, frozen or canned whole

Restless Rascals

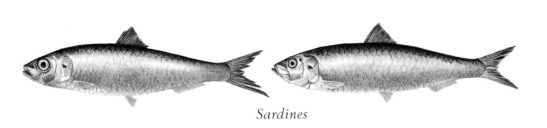

Sardines

fish names

Atlantic Herring
(*C. harengus*)

Pacific Herring
(*C. pallasi*)

Northern Anchovy
(*E. mordax*)

Pacific Sardine
(*S. sagax*): pilchard

Huge schools swim near the surface of the open ocean. In contrast to their Pacific cousins, Atlantic herring spawn over gravel or rocky bottoms. Their food sources are similar, and their predators include cods, striped bass, mackerel, tuna, salmon, sharks, squids, marine mammals, and sea birds, to name a few.

Pacific sardines grow to about a foot long. Their backs are bluish to dark green, with dark spots, and the undersides are light. They occur from Kamchatka to southeast Alaska to Guaymas in Mexico and south to Peru and Chile. These open ocean schools range from nearshore to hundreds of miles off the coast. They feed on plankton and are food for many species.

More than 135 species of **anchovies** occur nearshore—within 100 miles of the coastline— around the world. Some, like the northern anchovy which occurs from the Queen Charlotte Islands to Baja California and the Gulf of California, can live for seven years. Anchovy schools swim near the surface to more than a thousand feet down. These gregarious creatures eat zooplankton, copepods, arrow worms, krill, phytoplankton, small fishes, and their own eggs. They are eaten by fish, marine mammals, seabirds, and surely many other creatures.

fish fact

Menhaden, members of the herring family, provide the second largest amount of fish landed in the U.S.—1.7 billion pounds. But the entire catch is turned into fish oil, which we consume as a component of other foods, food supplements, or cooking oils—never as "fish."

HOW THEY'RE CAUGHT: Fishing for Pacific highly migratory species is managed by the Pacific Fishery Management Council, and by the states of California and Alaska. The federal plan delineates fishing limits for humans while considering the needs of ocean creatures that rely on these small fish for food themselves. The herring fishery off California is highly regulated, as is the nearshore fishery in Alaska. The latter two are fisheries for herring spawning on kelp or eelgrass, a highly valued species exported to Japan. Fishers catch these small fishes using nets, purse seines, gillnets, and trawls.

Anchovy

ON EATING THEM

When you eat chicken, shrimp or pork, you are also eating fish: Fish oil and fish meal (wild-caught sardines, herring, anchovies; and by-kill of other fish) make up 33 percent of the content of shrimp food; 20 percent of pig food; and 55 percent of the content of poultry food.

How They're Doing: These small pelagic fish wax and wane according to changes in oceanic conditions. In sparse years, overfishing these species is definitely possible given our industrial-strength fishing capability. The catastrophic collapse of the sardine fishery off the West Coast in the 1940s resulted in devastation of the Monterey canneries. Taking into account these cycles, at present Pacific and Atlantic herring are abundant. Sardines are abundant and increasing off the U.S. Pacific coast, and various U.S. anchovy populations appear to be faring well.

Special Issues: There is very little bycatch in the fisheries that target the huge, dense schools of these small fish.

Markets: The huge sardine canneries that handled fish in the boom off Monterey from the 1920s to 1940s no longer exist to process sardines in that form. The familiar "pizza" anchovies are not from the U.S. Primary exporting countries are Canada, the U.S., Norway, Iceland and Japan. The primary consumers of herring are Japan, the U.S. and northern Europe.

Can you can get the same health benefits by just taking fish oil capsules? NO.

When you eat fish, you not only get the benefits of Omega-3 fatty acids, you also take in less saturated fat than if you were otherwise to have eaten a higher-fat food. Fish oil capsules contain high levels of cholesterol. You won't get the same beneficial effect if you just use fish-oil capsules than if your diet contained fish. Also, fish-oil capsules contain vitamins A and D, which can be harmful in large amounts.

Bluefish

Bluefish

**OVERALL
RECOMMENDATION:**

*Bluefish fall in the YELLOW
zone of the Fish Scale because
they're widespread but
overfished.*

fish names

Bluefish
(P. saltatrix): chopper, snapper, blue

In the Wild: This feisty carnivore can be found following schools of squid or smaller fish from Maine to Florida, but can range as far north as Nova Scotia and south to Argentina. They're also found off the north coast of Africa, the Mediterranean, the Azores, Spain, Portugal, South Africa, New Zealand, and Australia. But as Alan Davidson so insightfully writes in his distinguished book *Seafood: A Connoisseur's Guide and Cookbook,* bluefish is a "prime example of a fish which has a very wide distribution, yet is thought of in certain places as being purely local. For anglers on the eastern seaboard of the USA, the 'blues' are 'theirs'."

Bluefish are very migratory along the coast, their journeys governed by movements of warm water and food. It's a spectacular sight to see an army of blues running their prey to the shoreline, the water seeming to boil in the feeding frenzy. Indeed, they give a spirited fight, and it certainly gets the surfcasters' blood pumping with "blitz fever" as they frenziedly search their surfbags for the perfect lure that matches the escaping prey.

Named for its color (certainly not its temperament)—blue-green above, silvery-white underneath—the bluefish is also known for its formidable teeth and cannibalistic tendencies. The latter could be why most schools of bluefish tend to be made up of similar-sized fish—since the bigger blues are prone to eating their smaller kin. Schools of blues in rare instances can extend for miles. They can live 12 years and grow to more than three feet and 30 pounds, but most are under 15 pounds.

Bluefish

 Bluefish: fresh; whole fish or fillets; smoked; smoked pâté

ON EATING THEM

Bluefish is excellent marinated and smoked, especially in the fall when the fish are more oily. You can also use cooked bluefish to make fish cakes or mock "crab" cakes, or even in sushi rolls to replace tuna.

NUTRITION: BLUEFISH

186 calories
6 g fat

Rich in Omega-3 fatty acids, protein, zinc, and B vitamins (including B6, B12 and Niacin). Like other fatty fish, bluefish is an excellent source of the fat-soluble vitamins A, D and K. Calorie and fat content based on a 3 oz. serving.

How They're Doing: Bluefish in U.S. waters are overfished and at relatively low abundance compared to the exceptional years they had in the 1980s. Bluefish is one of the very few fish for which fishing controls were put in place before problems began. Nonetheless, U.S. populations of bluefish have since declined for unclear reasons, possibly due to non-fishing factors which are difficult to pinpoint. While much reduced from previous highs, they're still widespread.

Special Issues: With most bluefish taken by hook and line, by-kill is minimal, though released fish suffer some mortality.

On Eating Them: Bluefish, especially the bigger ones, could be contaminated with PCBs. To minimize exposure, health officials recommend eating fish weighing less than six pounds and avoiding the dark red meat, skin, or organs.

HOW THEY'RE CAUGHT: Sport fishers are responsible for the vast majority of bluefish caught. Many of these are sold to wholesalers. Most commercial bluefish fishers use gillnets and trawls.

Lady M's Marinade:

Fillet and remove skin from fillets. Cut flesh in 3-4-inch wide strips.

Fill a big bowl half full with preferably low-salt soy sauce, a smidgen of water, and about three glugs of bottled lemon juice. Mix in a little bit (maybe 2 TBSP) of dark brown sugar; a handful of dried parsley; handful of dried oregano; half a handful of dried basil.

Peel and grate (or very finely chop) fresh ginger and mix it in the liquid. Sprinkle dried garlic powder (about 1 TBSP) or peel and finely chop fresh garlic into the bowl. Swirl it all together, and gently place raw fish strips into bowl, making sure everything's covered. Let soak overnight.

Smoke the next day to desired donenness. Be careful not to let it smoke too long, as it could get too dry. Smoked bluefish are great when a bit moist, and served on crackers. Smoked bluefish keeps well in the fridge for a couple of days, longer in the freezer, as the marinating and smoking process cures the flesh so its flavor is more stabilized.

Contributed by Mercédès Lee

Atlantic Hake

Hake/Whiting

Pacific Hake

Cape Hake

Atlantic & Silver Hake

OVERALL RECOMMENDATION:

Hake fall anywhere in the GREEN to YELLOW zone on the Fish Scale. Be careful about the hake you buy. The three Atlantic species reviewed here have problems, so they rate a YELLOW. On the other hand, Pacific hake and cape hake are doing fine–rating a GREEN – and can substitute for the other members of this family. Or, maybe you'll want to make a pasta salad with imitation crab made from hake-based surimi.

In the Wild: A confusing and multitudinous group if there ever was one, hakes are members of the codfish family *Gadidae* and exist as genetically different (but behaviorally and anatomically similar) species in both the Atlantic and Pacific oceans. Often referred to as whiting, they frequently swim together but they don't "school" in the real essence of the term. Schooling in fish implies evenly spaced fish pointing all in the same direction and moving as though they were a single organism. One could say hake swarm in dense aggregations, especially where food is concerned. These important predators feed on all manner of fish, shrimp, and squid. They have been known to strand themselves in pursuit of herring, especially come autumn. In turn, they're eaten by other fish, marine mammals, and seabirds. In one sense hake are wanderers, highly migratory as a matter of fact.

In the Gulf of Maine **silver hake** spawn in summer, in the place where haddock spawn in spring and pollock in autumn; to each its own time, indeed. Another population spawns from southern Georges Bank through the mid-Atlantic region. Silver hake typically grow to about 14 inches long, although they can get as big as 2 1/2 feet, and more than five pounds. Their silvery iridescent coloring and gold flecks fade upon death. But back onto the subject of the living, east coast whiting first breed at about two years old, and can live 10 years. Along the eastern seaboard, silver hake occur from Newfoundland to South Carolina. (Other hake species occur throughout the east Atlantic.)

Hake: fresh; smoked; fillets; protein paste for surimi and other food products; imitation crab

European Hake

Atlantic Hake *(M. hubbsi)*: Argentine hake, silver hake (but not to be confused with *M. bilinearis* in West Atlantic waters)

Silver Hake *(M. bilinearis)*: Atlantic hake (but not to be confused with *M. hubbsi* in East Atlantic waters), whiting, to be distinguished from other species like red hake which are not in the *Merluccius* family

Pacific Hake *(M. productus)*: whiting

Cape Hake *(M.capensis)*: cape capensis

Chilean Hake *(M. gay gayi)*: English hake, offshore silver hake

In the Pacific, both hakes (*M. productus* and *M. capensis*) occur anywhere from Baja California to British Columbia, and their "schools" can stretch in a lense-like configuration up to 12 miles long, seven miles wide, and 20 feet deep. Pacific hake live almost twice as long as their Atlantic counterparts, aging to 20 years, and maturing at a little more than four years old. Other *Merluccius* hakes besides those detailed here are found in the South Pacific and South Atlantic oceans, off South America, South Africa, and Namibia.

How They're Doing: Catches in all parts of the world have been increasing since the early 1990s. The northern population of silver hake appears to be holding its own for now, but the southern separate breeding population for unknown reasons continues to decline. Off the Pacific coast of the U.S., hake populations have been on the upswing since the mid-1990s. Scientists don't know how natural environmental fluctuations, like El Niño and La Niña, affect them.

Red Hake

HOW THEY'RE CAUGHT: All of the hake species mentioned above are fished with trawl gear. Three types of processors are active in the Pacific: "motherships," which process but do not catch fish; catcher-processors, which do both; and shore-based processors. On the U.S. east coast, the silver hake fishery regulations are interwoven with the groundfish regulations. As members of this troubled group, hake are among the species managers are trying to recover by cutting catches. A controversial new market and fishery for small silver hake recently developed in New England and managers are concerned about growing incentives to catch juveniles that were previously ignored.

In the southern hemisphere, responsible management regimes for hake are in place for fish that come out of South Africa and Namibia, but less so for South America.

On Eating Them: The hake taken off the coasts of Washington and Oregon go almost entirely to manufacture surimi, a protein paste made by chopping and processing the fish and then making it into fish paste used in many foods in Japan, or into imitation crab meat sold in the U.S. Pacific hake contain a parasite that produces an enzyme which softens the flesh of the fish. For this reason, they have to be processed and frozen quickly.

Special Issues: By-kill, especially of salmon and rockfish, used to be a concern in the Pacific hake fishery, but recent measures have been successful in reducing by-kill substantially. On average, the gear now used hauls 99 percent hake (only one percent by-kill).

NUTRITION: WHITING

110 calories
25 fat calories
3 g total fat
70 mg cholesterol
19 g protein
calcium 6%

(Based on a 3 oz. serving size. Vitamins and minerals are based on 2,000 calorie diet.)

FISH CONSUMPTION

In 1998, 986.6 million pounds of salmon, sardines, tuna, and clams were canned for human consumption. That same year, the U.S. canned 544.3 million pounds of fish (primarily spot, sardines, and the by-kill and by-product of other fishing and fish processing) for petfood.

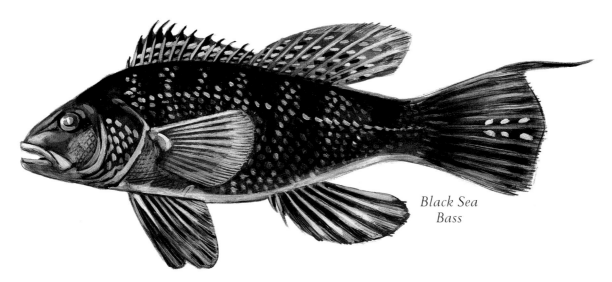

Black Sea Bass

Bass

Fish
Scale

← Striped Bass

In the Wild: **Black sea bass** are found all along the U.S. Atlantic coast from northern Florida to Cape Cod, being very common in Chesapeake Bay. It's a gray, dusky brown, or blackish fish highlighted by beautiful blue streaks, with particularly pronounced scales and spiky fins. It likes the rocky bottom and prefers to hang out around jetties and ship-wrecks. Any black sea bass seen under 12 inches will undoubtedly be female. But any over a foot long will be male. This is because, in an odd twist of nature, they change sex, from female to male when they get older. Surprisingly, or perhaps not, Aristotle was the first to make this observation around 300 B.C. Reaching a full two feet long, black sea bass can live—at this point as males—to at most 15 years old. They migrate eastward to overwinter offshore at the edge of the continental shelf where the temperatures are much more friendly for them. Unlike some fish, they find food visually, feeding on crabs, lobsters, mussels, small fish, and the like. They spawn mainly from March to October, with the southern fish repro-ducing earlier than the northern fish.

There are two versions of **striped bass**: wild and farmed. And they are indeed different ani-mals. Farmed striped bass are a cross between striped bass and white bass (making *Morone sax-atilis x Morone chrysops*). They are reared to a size of two to five pounds for market. Wild ones are anadromous, meaning they spawn in estuaries or rivers and spend most of the rest of their lives in more oceanic environments. They have greenish backs, white bellies, and sport solid black lines along their flanks. A broken striped pattern and slightly stubbier shape differen-tiates a farmed striped bass from its wild counterpart. Wild fish migrate extensively along the

Black Sea Bass: whole; fresh or frozen; skinless fillets; live market
 (for ethnic markets in the United States and Canada)
Striped Bass: Half sold are farmed

OVERALL RECOMMENDATION:

GREEN on the Fish Scale for striped bass; RED for black sea bass because they're overfished and depleted. Try substituting the lat-ter with the former. Strong man-agement produced recovery of wild striped bass.

fish names

Black Sea Bass
(*C. striata*)

Striped Bass
(*M. saxatilis*): bass, striper, rockfish, cow (large female)

Black Sea
Bass

Atlantic close to the coast and are found from the Gulf of St. Lawrence to northern Florida and also in the Gulf of Mexico. It has a long, illustrious reputation as a fine-eating and good-fighting fish. Striped bass are clearly generalists: they're not picky eaters and they range quite far in their travels for food and procreation. Regarding the former, they eat a wide range of shellfish and other fish. The oldest and largest fish tend to be females. A large female striped bass can produce one- to two-million eggs in a single season. (But very few of them survive, of course.) If allowed, they can live more than 30 years and grow six feet long; a big Cow indeed. "Cow," by the way, is a term of endearment given by admiring fishers to big female striped bass.

The tributaries of the Chesapeake Bay constitute the major stronghold for striped bass spawning along the mid-Atlantic coast. Interestingly, striped bass were also introduced to California around 1880 and seemed to thrive there for more than a century. However, they're not as migratory as their East Coast brethren and growing pollution problems from sewage and agriculture seem to be taking a serious toll as there are fewer and fewer young bass surviving.

How They're Doing:
Black sea bass are overfished and depleted. Striped bass recently recovered from severe depletion in the 1980s, caused by overfishing and exacerbated by poor water quality in spawning and nursery habitats in the Chesapeake Bay and Hudson River systems. A recovery program designed in the mid-1980s allowed females to spawn at least once. This brought successful successive generations. Striped bass were formally declared restored in 1995, and their recovery is frequently highlighted as a model of successful fisheries management.

Special Issues:
Continued expansion of striped bass farming could have more serious ecological costs than what we currently see, but at present it's dominated by low impact closed systems, which is good (see Farming Ocean Life, page 60). By-kill in the wild fishery is low. For black sea bass, habitat concerns are significant because of heavy trawling for other species occurs in their living area. Because black sea bass are caught in a mixed-species fishery (meaning together with other fish), there are some bycatch concerns.

"The [striped] basse is one of the best fishes in the country, and though men are soon wearied with other fish, yet are they never with basse."

—*Wood, 1634*

**NUTRITION:
STRIPED BASS**

97 calories
21 fat calories
2.3 g total fat
80 mg cholesterol
17.7 g protein

(Based on a 3 oz. serving size.)

HOW THEY'RE CAUGHT: Black sea bass are caught in trawls, traps, or fish pots. There also is a significant recreational fishery. Fishing regulations prohibit new entrants to the commercial fishery, set gear restrictions, minimum fish sizes, and separate commercial and recreational catch limits. Fishing occurs year-round, with most activity from spring to fall.

Wild striped bass are caught primarily by recreational fishers, taking in fact three times more than the commercial fishery in 1996. Wild striped bass are caught commercially principally with gillnets. There are about 100 fish farms in the U.S. and they use ponds, tanks, and closed systems to rear the hybrid fish that is a cross between wild striped bass and white bass.

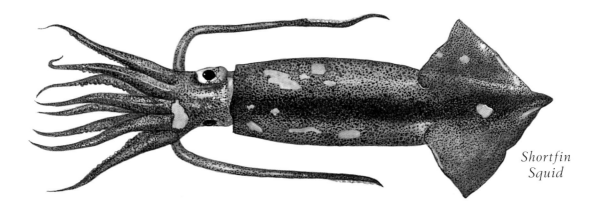

*Shortfin
Squid*

Squid

In the Wild: Squid are cephalopods, kin to the octopus, cuttlefish, and chambered nautilus. Slimy creatures, squid seem without substance when handled out of water, belying their true, complex natures in their underwater universe. These animals have an extensive nervous system and the most complex brain of any invertebrate animal. All three species profiled here grow to about a foot long and live at most a year and a half. But a full life it is.

Many squid species exist worldwide from shallow bays to abyssal depths. Highly migratory, they spend most of their time in the open sea. They undertake vertical migration, in which during daylight hours they swim down deep, coming up to feed at night. They move through the water by using their two fins and a siphon that jet propels them in any direction. When they're alarmed or otherwise emotionally excited, their colors flash from opal to orange to ivory, with pulses of gold, green, and red appropriate to the occasion. They have eight arms and two feeding tentacles at the end of an elongated body, covering an internal shell. They use their tentacles to grab prey (some squids are equipped with little hooks). Some also inject a poison to kill their prey. Their mouth is equipped with a sharp beak for tearing and crushing their food. To procreate, a male places his sperm sacks to the oviduct of a receptive female. They continue to swim together until the female lays her 200 or so newly fertilized eggs and carefully covers them in a protective jelly. She takes her arms and carefully attaches her elongated egg pouch to the sea floor, sometimes on egg pouches laid by other female squid. The pair repeats this several times within a short period. From what we know, they die after mating.

 Squid: sold as calamari; fresh; frozen whole; frozen cleaned; frozen tubes; rings and tentacles; or canned in ink or tomato sauce

**OVERALL
RECOMMENDATION:**

*Squid from the Atlantic rate a
YELLOW on the Fish Scale
because they're overfished.
YELLOW if Pacific, due to
lack of management.*

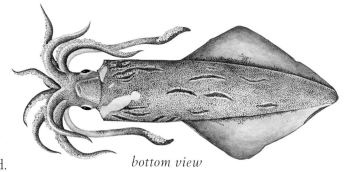

The market squid, *Loligo opalescens*, occurs from Alaska to Baja California. The northern shortfin, *Ilex illecebrosus*, ranges from Labrador to Florida, while the longfin inshore squid, *Loligo pealei*, can be found in schools from Newfoundland to the Gulf of Venezuela. There are numerous other species throughout the world.

bottom view

How They're Doing:
Squid off the east coast U.S. (*Ilex* and *Loligo*) are numerous but overfished. This means that if fishing continues at the current pace, the squid will not sustain the pressure and they'll become more and more depleted. Market squid off the U.S. Pacific coast are again abundant after the warm waters of El Niño reduced their numbers.

Their short life span, combined with rapid growth, early maturity and year-round spawning make the squid able to withstand heavy fishing pressure. At the same time, since squid generations do not overlap, it is possible to take too many of the animals that are of catchable size in one season—the same as the ones that are the age for spawning. This characteristic and their vulnerability to environmental and oceanographic conditions make for extreme short-term fluctuations in population size and distribution.

fish names

Longfin Squid
(*L. pealei*): winter squid

Shortfin Squid (*I. illecebrosus*): summer squid

Market Squid
(*L. opalescens*): California market squid

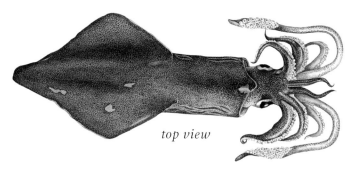
top view

Special Issues:
By-kill is sometimes problematic, sometimes low to non-existent where the squid school only among themselves. That squid are caught close to the surface also make habitat problems neglible.

HOW THEY'RE CAUGHT: As restrictions get tighter for other fisheries along the east coast, fishers increasingly take up squid fishing. From Canada to North Carolina fishers catch squid with trawl gear, pound nets, and traps. From June to September, trawlers take shortfin squid near the edge of the continental shelf. From October to March they catch longfin squid offshore, and from April to September they catch them inshore. Federal regulators control fishing for squid via permits, catch limits, and restrictions on the type of gear that can be used.

On the west coast, fishers catch squid using purse seines or round haul nets set out at night with high intensity lamps to lure the squid up from deep water. Fishing for squid coincides with concentrations of the animals when breeding in semi-protected bays. Fishers catch squid in Monterey Bay (May through October), and off southern California (September through March), all within state waters.

Elsewhere around the world, particularly in the Asian-Pacific region, fishers frequently use jigs as well as other gear types to catch squid.

Atlantic
Mackerel

Mackerel

In the Wild: Mackerels are kin to tunas in the family *Scrombridae*. With numerous species of mackerel throughout the world, they're considered one of the top predators in many oceans and coastal zones. They're remarkably fast-moving fish—swimming up to 70 miles an hour—that migrate in large schools over great distances, moving inshore and offshore seasonally. As with many other fish, changes in water temperature seem to trigger their movements in the spring and fall. Consistent with the larger tunas, the first dorsal fin (the top fin closest to the head) of mackerels retracts into a groove, making them nearly perfectly streamlined for fast, agile swimming. Indeed, mackerels are heavily muscled predators, with predominantly red, well-oxygenated muscles designed for quick bursts of speed. In an unusual adaptation, those in the genus *Scomber* have two transluscent membranes covering the front and rear parts of their eye which open and close, serving in essence as eyelids. This protective covering allows them to keep their underwater world in view even when their eyelids are closed.

OVERALL RECOMMENDATION:

All these mackerels fall in the GREEN zone of the Fish Scale primarily because they're abundant despite historically poor management. Take note, though, that fishing for king mackerel remains poorly managed in the Gulf of Mexico.

Atlantic mackerels range from Labrador to North Carolina, with two separate breeding populations—a southern group that spawns in the mid-Atlantic in the spring, and a separate northern group that spawns later in the Gulf of St. Lawrence. Others occur in the Mediterranean, Black Sea, off Iceland, and Norway. Living as long as 20 years, they mature at around three. Atlantic mackerels are fast growing fish. They can get as big as 20 inches long and three pounds. The young eat plankton and fish eggs, and the adults eat plankton, copepods, squids, herrings, and sandlances.

fish fact

Mackerels in the genus *Scomber* have a nictitating membrane akin to an eyelid.

Mackerel: In U.S.: fresh; frozen; smoked. In Brazil: fresh; salted; and canned.

Chub mackerel, called Pacific mackerel off the West Coast, occupy a wide range of ocean expanse: from the Atlantic (farther south than the Atlantic mackerel as far as Cuba), and throughout the Pacific and Indian Oceans. Pacific chub mackerels have a clear whitish belly, differing from the Atlantic chubs which sport spots below their midline. Indeed, their electric blue color and black lines take your breath away if you're lucky enough to see them in their wild glory. Chubs grow fast—meaning they reach their maximum size early in life—around two feet. A chub mackerel can live more than 10 years, and they begin reproducing when they're about three. Subtropical waters are good for chubs in that they seem to be able to spawn year-round there. Elsewhere, their spawning occurs when the waters have warmed a bit, from early spring through summer. Their numbers fluctuate—sometimes radically—in response to swings in water temperatures caused by El Niño and other related weather phenomena. Large schools sweep along the Pacific coast, following concentrations of food. As one guidebook attests: "This mackerel has the most catholic of tastes and will snap eagerly at anything offered..." In the wild—as opposed to being lured by dry flies and sparerib bones which they do indeed go after—chubs feast on zooplankton, squid, and small fish. Likewise, California sea lions, northern fur seals, bald eagles, and terns eat them.

Most **king mackerel** caught are about 10 pounds. One Florida record logged in at 90 pounds, a true rarity. Female *S. cavalla* grow faster and larger than the males. They mature around four years old and can live more than 10 years. Three identified populations of king mackerel exist: Gulf of Mexico, South Atlantic (off Florida), and one off the coast of Brazil. Highly predatious, they use the high-speed surprise approach to attack schools of squid, herring, menhaden, and other fishes.

NUTRITION: MACKEREL

210 calories
120 fat calories
13 g total fat
60 mg cholesterol
21 g protein
Iron 5%

(Based on a 3 oz. serving size. Vitamins and minerals are based on 2,000 calorie diet.)

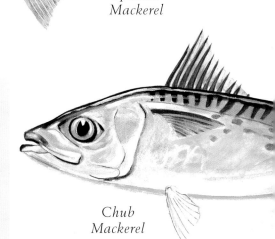

Spanish Mackerel

Chub Mackerel

HOW THEY'RE CAUGHT: Commercial and recreational fishers catch mackerels pretty much throughout their range. Depending on the species and location, commercial fishers use purse seines, trawls, gillnets or pound nets to catch them. European fleets use industrial-size trawlers equipped with freezers that allow them in one fell-swoop to catch and process the fish on-board. The size, strength, speed, and power of king mackerel make them a favored gamefish in the southern U.S. Recreational anglers catch nearly twice the amount of king mackerel than do commercial fishers.

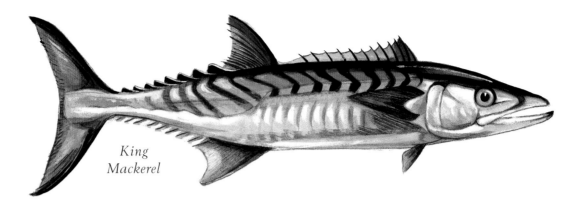

King Mackerel

Atlantic Mackerel
(S. scombrus)

Chub Mackerel
(S. japonicus):
Pacific mackerel

King Mackerel
(S. cavalla): kingfish, old mossback

Spanish Mackerel
(S. maculatus)

Cero *(S. regalis)*: painted mackerel

Wahoo *(A. solandri)*: ono

Spanish mackerel range throughout the Atlantic and Gulf of Mexico. These fish are silvery-colored with gold spots. They occur from the Chesapeake Bay south to Brazil. Occasionally they wander as far north as Cape Cod. Their coastal migrations go like this: spending October to March off Florida, by April they reach the Carolinas, move into the Chesapeake Bay by May, and arrive in Narragansett Bay by July. They reach a maximum of 20 pounds, but more commonly they're around ten pounds. They eat mostly menhaden.

Cero, also known as painted mackerel, differ from other mackerels in their dot and dash gold markings. They're typically five to 10 pounds. Cero occur from Cape Cod to Brazil, but are most abundant in south Florida and the West Indies.

Wahoo is the only one of the mackerels that prefers solitude. They occur in the Atlantic from Maryland south to northern South America and throughout the Gulf of Mexico. Typically they grow to about 20 pounds. A distinguishing feature from the other mackerels are their jaws; they're beak-like, and both the upper and lower portions move.

How They're Doing: There are as many Atlantic mackerel now as there ever have been, but, in a curious anomaly, the size of the fish and how fast they grow is decreasing. Chub mackerel are doing well overall. King mackerel in the Gulf of Mexico are overfished, not having yet recovered from the serious depletion caused by unregulated fishing in the 1980s. The population off the southeastern U.S. is not overfished. Spanish mackerel are increasing in both the Gulf and the Atlantic after years of overfishing because of the attention they're now getting from managers. Both cero and wahoo are in good shape.

Special Issues: Some mackerel fisheries entail by-kill of other sea creatures because of the fishing gear used to catch them. Wahoo are sometimes indvertently caught on longlines targeting other species.

ON EATING THEM

Mackerel is an oily fish high in Omega-3 fatty acids, which provide some health benefits. Mackerels, and all scombroid fishes, must be iced immediately upon being caught, and handled carefully to prevent bacteria-related toxins from developing.

The Leapers
Salmon

INGREDIENTS

4 wild Alaska salmon fillets, approximately 6 ozs. each

white wine

fish stock

1 TBSP finely chopped shallots

chanterelles (you may also substitute black trumpet mushrooms)

juice of ½ of a lemon

½ tsp Dijon mustard

¼ cup heavy cream

1 TBSP fresh herbs, preferably chervil

Wild Alaska Salmon and Chanterelles

Carefully clean mushrooms and cook in a little butter. When you observe them giving off some liquid, drain the mushrooms and save the juice. Please note that certain mushrooms such as chanterelles and black trumpets give off a lot of juice.

Place wild Alaska salmon fillets in a sauteuse with a tight-fitting cover. Add a combination of wine and stock to reach about half way up the wild salmon. Add the shallots and the mushroom juice that has been set aside. Cover tightly and cook over a medium heat for about 3-4 minutes. Wild salmon should be very slightly cooked, that is, rare inside. Remove salmon pieces and keep warm.

In same pot add chanterelles and reduce liquid by half. Add lemon, mustard, and cream. Bring to a boil and reduce until lightly thickened. Season to taste with salt and additional lemon if necessary. Add fresh herbs.

Place wild Alaska salmon on warm plates. Pour sauce and chanterelles over wild fish. Garnish with seasonal vegetables.

Contributed by chef David Waltuck of the restaurant Chanterelle in New York City.

Atlantic Salmon

Salmon

Fish
Scale

**OVERALL
RECOMMENDATION:**

*GREEN on the Fish Scale for wild
Alaskan salmon because they're abundant,
their habitat is intact, and their fisheries are well-
managed. RED for Atlantic salmon and other farmed
imports because of associated disease and habitat problems. On the West Coast, wild salmon are severely depleted and rate a RED; likewise hatchery-raised salmon rate a
RED on the Fish Scale because of the competition, disease,
and habitat problems they cause for their wild
brethren. There are some Atlantic salmon farmers,
most notably in Maine, that rotate their fish pens
to reduce disease, pollution, and predation
problems. We rate these a YELLOW
on the Fish Scale.*

In the Wild: Active and aggressive predators, all salmon frequent
cold, rushing streams, estuaries, and the upper levels of the ocean.
They are born in fresh water, and return as adults to spawn in the
same gravel bottomed streams where they hatched. Salmon are
native only to the northern hemisphere, and were once found
throughout the entire Pacific Rim, northern Europe and into
Russia. Today, introduced populations of salmon inhabit the
Great Lakes, South America, and New Zealand, and introduced
Atlantic species are found in the Pacific. Steelhead trout—in the
same genus as Pacific salmon—is usually classified as a salmon
because it's highly oceanic.

The **Atlantic salmon** (*Salmo salar*—the leaping leaper) can still be found
in small numbers in the wild in Maine, maritime Canada, the Faroe Islands,
Greenland, the British Isles, Russia, and a few places in Europe. It is a silver
skinned fish with cross-like spots over the body and head, with a nearly white underside.
While most other salmon spawn once and die, wild Atlantic salmon return to natal streams
more than once to spawn.

Salmon are named after, and understood by, the watershed in which they're born and to
which they'll return, and the season they ascend—for example, Sacramento River winter chi-

 Atlantic, Chinook and Coho Salmon: fresh or frozen whole fish; steaks; fillets; smoked
Chum, Pink and Sockeye Salmon: canned; smoked
Steelhead: fresh; frozen; fillets; canned; smoked

Wild
Alaskan
Salmon

Pen-rotated
Farmed
Salmon

Atlantic
Salmon

West Coast
Wild Salmon

Hatchery-
raised Salmon

nooks. Each year, six species of North American Pacific salmon and steelhead return to tens of thousands of streams that flow from Alaska and the Pacific Northwest's temperate rainforests into the fjords and estuaries of this rich region. When it comes time for their spawning run, salmon that have ranged as far as 2,500 miles from the mouths of their birth-rivers turn toward home for the first and final time. There is no equivocation; an adult salmon's homeward migration is rapid and direct, averaging about thirty miles per day. Fish that have spread over thousands of square ocean miles converge, arriving at their natal rivers within days of each other, guided by sophisticated internal navigation systems using the sun and Earth's magnetic field.

Their olfactory sense is extraordinarily acute, allowing them to smell their tiny natal springs flowing into major rivers.

Salmon usually cease eating by the time they enter their natal streams. If not caught by fishers first, they must battle up thundering waterfalls, rapids, and fish ladders—traveling hundreds, even thousands, of miles inland on an empty stomach. The males arrive as gaunt, hooked-jaw hump-backs. By then, male and female alike have large white patches of bruised skin on their backs and sides. Virtually all Pacific salmon except a few steelheads die after spawning, even those that breed in low reaches near the sea. The hunting and foraging movements of many other animals—including bears, eagles, coastal wolves, and numerous others—are coordinated with salmon spawning.

When the tributary of their own birth is finally attained, salmon will seek out suitable gravel—clean and of the appropriate size—to dig their nests, called redds. The female turns on her side, presses her tail to the bottom, and with powerful flexes lifts sand, debris, and gravel into the current. Her vigorous digging is interspersed by periods of resting, while she evaluates her progress with her fins. Her nest-making activities attract suitors. While the female continues to excavate, the accepted male courts her with repeated touches—his snout to her flanks—and by crossing over her tail and then quivering his body against hers. Eventually the pair will lie side by side with bellies close together near the bottom of the nest. After the male deposits his milt (sperm) over her roe (eggs), the female rakes her tail back and forth to cover the redd with loose gravel. Then the process continues a short distance upstream, until as many as seven nests have been built. Salmon lay only about two to five thousand eggs; in contrast, some some marine

SALMON IN NATIVE CULTURE

The native tribes of the Northwest became the richest people in North America, having wandered into a region replete with teeming salmon. Living as they did amid the world's richest natural salmon "factories," the people built their culture around the fishes. All houses faced the water. The salmon were plenty enough to draw tribes from a wide region into trade. For travel offshore, dugout canoes up to sixty feet in length were sent against the seas. These creatures of the water, salmon became family crests or spirit helpers, their images carved into everything from totem poles to food bowls, woven into baskets, painted on possessions, tattooed upon one's very flesh, and everywhere incorporated into the patterns of life. Wrote John Jewett, who lived among the Moachat Nootka for two years after being taken captive in 1803: "There are few people more expert in the art of fishing. Such is the immense quantity of these fish, and they are taken with such facility, that I have known upwards of twenty-five hundred brought into Maquinnas house at once." The natives developed many methods of taking salmon, including trolling with hook and line, spearing, netting, and trapping. Various traps included a particularly cunning crib set at the foot of a waterfall, into which salmon fell back after an unsuccessful attempt at leaping the fall.

—Adapted from
Song for the Blue Ocean, *by Carl Safina*

fishes lay millions. But compared to the tiny eggs that most marine fishes abandon to near-certain death, salmon eggs are relatively enormous and carefully deposited. Consequently, salmon hatch as robust babies with big yolk sacs that provides a ready food source for them to grow for weeks within the gravel's relative safety.

Sockeye Salmon

After emergence, young salmon spend varying lengths of time in fresh water before moving toward the ocean. When the time comes for the young fish to make their saltwater debut, they undergo a dramatic transformation in body shape, coloration, and physiology to prepare them for the ocean. Helped along by high river flows of spring snow melt, young ocean-bound salmon are washed out of their natal streams, pointing into the current and traveling backwards on a sea-bound journey that will take anywhere from a few days to several months.

The **chinook** or **king salmon** is the largest, averaging 15 to 30 pounds , with giants that go more than 100 pounds. Its silver back and tail are spotted with round black markings, and colored glue-green to black. Kings can be found from mid-California to the Arctic, Bering Sea, and into northern Japan. They mature when they're about four years old. They migrate tremendous distances. The **coho** ranges from California to the sub-arctic, and weighs four to 16 pounds. **Sockeye** are the mainstay of the commercial industry and the most valuable salmon species in the U.S. Sockeye, with their bluish-green speckled backs mature at four years, typically reaching seven pounds, but the largest recorded weighed more than 15 pounds. Sockeye, by the way, are the salmon that develop the most extremely hooked jaw during spawning and turn a deep red. The smallest and most abundant salmon, **pink salmon**, range from southern California up through Puget Sound to British Columbia, into southeastern Alaska, across the Arctic and as far as Japan and Korea. They mature around two years old and weigh up to six pounds. Unlike other salmon, **pinks** spawn at the high-tide line, not upriver. It is the pronounced hump that males develop at spawning time that gives these salmon their nickname of Humpback. **Chum** or **dog salmon** become mature when they're between three and six years old, and weigh from eight to 12 pounds. In their days, chum salmon occurred from Del Mar, California, through Oregon to the Alaskan Arctic, and west to Honshu, Japan. They are now extinct from central Oregon south.

NUTRITION: SALMON

130-180 calories (depending on species)
35-80 fat calories
total fat 4-9 g
50-75 mg cholesterol
22-23 g protein

(Based on a 3 oz. serving size. Vitamins and minerals are based on 2,000 calorie diet.)

fish names

Atlantic Salmon (*S. salar*)

Chum Salmon (*O. keta*): dog, or chum Dog

Coho Salmon (*O. kisutch*): silver salmon

King Salmon (*O. tshawytscha*): Chinook salmon

Pink Salmon (*O. gorbuscha*): humpbacks

Sockeye Salmon (*O. nerka*): reds

Steelhead Trout (*O. mykiss*): rainbow trout

How They're Doing: Salmon that return to rivers in Alaska remain abundant, mainly because the habitat that supports them is still intact, with the rivers clean and healthy and able to sustain salmon eggs and support young salmon.

Wild Pacific salmon from central British Columbia south are in trouble due to dams and land abuses that pollute streams with sediments and chemicals, such as clear-cut logging, farm runoff, and overgrazing. Pacific salmon have disappeared from about 40 percent of their historical breeding ranges in Washington, Oregon, Idaho, and California over the last century. Numerous populations that originate in rivers in Washington, Oregon, and California are listed as endangered over much of their range; some populations have gone extinct. Wild Atlantic salmon are severely depleted throughout their range, and many populations are endangered; some are extinct.

On Eating Them: Be aware that drugs, antibiotics, vaccines, disinfectants, and pesticides are usually used in the process of farming and hatchery-raising salmon to control contaminants and infectious diseases that are inherent in the process. The Food and Drug Administration approves drugs that can be used in U.S. operations. The Environmental Protection Agency regulates the pesticides and algacides (to control algae) used in aquaculture. In many cases there is a "withdrawal" period whereby the animals are quarantined in clean water to flush out these additives from their systems before releasing them or bringing them to market.

HOW THEY'RE CAUGHT: In Alaska, and most other places, how many salmon fishers are allowed to catch is based on estimates of how many fish will return to spawn, and the fishery does not start until sufficient fish have passed upriver. King salmon are taken with seines, gillnets, or trolled lines. Chums and sockeyes are taken primarily with seines or gillnets. Coho are taken largely by hook and line. Pinks are occasionally taken by trollers, but mostly caught with gillnets and seines.

Managers regulate these fisheries in the Pacific Northwest by seasons, gear type, size restrictions, and catch limits. That few salmon now return to their natal rivers has all but eliminated fishing for wild salmon in much of the area from central California through central British Columbia since the late 1990s. Nonetheless, some fishing for hatchery-originated fish continues. Before being released into the wild, hatchery workers clip the fins of these fish to enable fishers to distinguish wild from hatchery-raised fish. When commercial fishers catch a salmon, they look to see if it has a clipped fin. If they're not supposed to catch wild salmon, either because the fishing season is closed or they're endangered, they can easily tell if it should be returned to sea or kept. A significant number of wild fish caught and returned to sea do die, so it's clearly not a perfect system.

Atlantic salmon are farmed in more than a dozen countries. Salmon have been introduced into the temperate southern hemisphere, including New Zealand and South America, from which many are then exported to northern markets. Last but not least, salmon are highly valued by recreational fishers from California to Alaska, and in Maine, Canada, and the British Isles.

Steelheads are one of the most widely introduced fishes around the world, and several countries report these unnaturally occurring hatchery fish caused diseases and ecological problems for native fish.

fish fact

In historic times, salmon canneries used the oil from salmon waste by-products as a substitute for diesel fuel to run the cannery motors.

Special Issues: In addition to being heavily fished, salmon are taken as by-kill in other fisheries. But the major problem for salmon on the Pacific coast is loss of habitat from logging (which clogs streams with silt), dams (which block passage and disrupt natural stream flows), intensive water use, agricultural practices (causing runoff of silt, fertilizers, and pesticides), and other development activities that affect the freshwater streams on which these fish highly depend. Because habitat destruction, not overfishing, is the driving factor in the declines of West Coast salmon, fishers are the chief economic force for salmon conservation. For those reasons, not buying legally caught wild West Coast salmon will do little to help salmon's long-term prospects, even though many of them are in terrible trouble.

Markets: Japan is the world's top consumer of salmon. The U.S., Japan, Canada, and Russia are major exporters of wild salmon. The main sources of farmed Atlantic salmon are the U.S., the United Kingdom, Chile, Norway, Canada, Ireland, and Iceland. Principal consumers of farmed Atlantic salmon in particular are Japan, the U.S., England, France, Sweden, Singapore, China, and Belgium. The shift in consumer preference from wild to farmed salmon during the 1990s had a tremendous impact on their price and on how many the U.S. exported.

HATCHERY VS. FARMED SALMON

Artificial reproduction of salmon includes hatchery-born and farmed.

Hatcheries hatch the fish and release them into streams at young ages. If they survive, they go to sea and later return. Farms raise the fish in captivity and send them to market when they are large enough. To breed Atlantic salmon, U.S. farmers many times import the milt (fish sperm) of salmon from Europe. The milt is used to fertilize the eggs of U.S. bred Atlantic salmon. Farm-raised fish are never released, except accidentally—and these are called "escapees."

Hatchery salmon compete with wild salmon and depress their survival, but then often do not survive well themselves. Salmon farms have caused water pollution and diseases that harm wild salmon. In the late 1990s, Washington State classified Atlantic salmon that escaped from farms there as a "pollutant," harmful to native salmon.

THE TOP CONSUMED SEAFOOD IN THE U.S.

(consumer preference based on consumption per capita)

1998	1995
1. tuna	1. shrimp
2. shrimp	2. cod
3. Alaska pollock	3. pollock
4. salmon	4. catfish
5. cod	5. scallops
6. catfish	6. salmon
7. clams	7. flounder
8. crabs	8. oysters
9. flounder/sole	9. orange roughy
10. halibut	10. mackerel
11. oysters	11. ocean perch

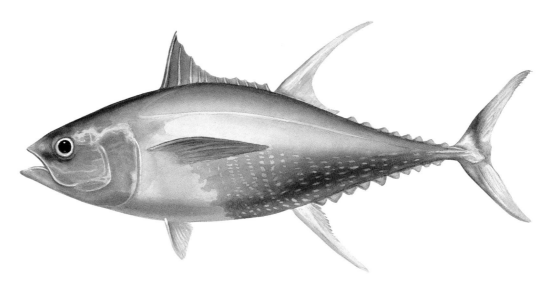

Sardinian Ahi

SERVES 4

INGREDIENTS

1 to 2 lbs fresh ahi
(yellowfin tuna), sliced in
about 1-inch steaks

1 cup olive oil

1 cup lemon juice

8 cloves garlic

2 TBSP fresh Italian parsley
(flat-leaf parsley),
chopped

1-2 tsp sea salt

Mix olive oil, lemon juice, garlic, parsley, and salt.

Pour marinade over ahi and let sit for at least three hours.

Heat grill to point where coals are glowing red.

Cook ahi on grill, no more than 2 minutes per side. (It is very important not to overcook.)

Serve at once on a bed of julienned fresh vegetables lightly sauteed in olive oil (vegetables may include leeks, zucchini, sweet peppers, and carrots).

This is absolutely the best recipe for ahi I have ever had. It is important that the fillets be thin to absorb the marinade, but this also makes them highly susceptible to overcooking.

Contributed by Pat Tummons

Macho Migrants

Mahimahi • Sharks • Swordfish • Tunas

SERVES 4-6

INGREDIENTS

The fish

1 pound firm, fresh mahimahi fillets

Chermoulla Dressing

2 garlic cloves, minced or pressed

1 TBSP ground paprika

1 TBSP ground cumin

2 tsp ground coriander

½ teaspoon red pepper flakes

1 to 2 fresh chiles, chopped with seeds

¼ cup chopped fresh cilantro

¼ cup fresh lemon juice

¼ cup olive oil

salt to taste

Couscous Salad

1 cup quick-cooking couscous

½ tsp salt

pinch of saffron

1 ⅓ cups boiling water

4 to 6 artichoke hearts, drained and cut into quarters (14-ounce can)

1 cucumber, peeled and sliced

1 tomato, cut into bite-sized wedges

1 orange, peeled and sliced crosswise into rounds

8 to 12 kalamata olives

a few lemon wedges

several fresh cilantro sprigs

Mahimahi & Chermoulla Couscous Salad

As a first course, lunch, or light dinner, this festive and colorful salad offers an irresistible combination of textures and tastes. Fresh mahimahi, marinated and sautéed in the powerful flavors of the Chermoulla sauce, is served with light and aromatic couscous and cool, refreshing garnishes.

Chermoulla Dressing is very hot and spicy. We recommend starting with one chile, tasting the dressing, and adding another if you like (or dare).

Rinse and drain the fish and set it aside. Combine all of the dressing ingredients in a blender or food processor and whirl until smooth. Place the drained fish in a bowl, cover with the dressing, and marinate in the refrigerator for about one hour.

Place the couscous, salt, and saffron in a heat-proof bowl. Pour in the boiling water, cover lightly, and side aside for about five minutes. Uncover and fluff with a fork to break up any lumps, then set aside (see note).

Transfer the mahimahi and its marinade into a lightly oiled skillet. Sauté on medium heat for about 10 minutes, turning once, until the flesh is firm and opaque, then remove the skin and flake with a fork.

To serve, spread the couscous on a large serving platter. Arrange the mahimahi in the middle surrounded by the artichoke hearts, cucumber slices, tomato wedges, orange rounds, and olives. Drizzle the marinade over the top and garnish with lemon wedges and cilantro.

Serve the salad warm or at room temperature.

Note: If you plan to serve the dish warm rather than at room temperature, cover the couscous when you set it aside so it will retain heat.

Reprinted with permission from: The Moosewood Restaurant Daily Special, by the Moosewood Collective. Clarkson Potter, New York, 1999.

Mahimahi

Mahimahi

OVERALL RECOMMENDATION:

GREEN on the Fish Scale, but by-kill on longlines and being new targets by longliners warrant concern. Its current abundance and reproductive capability, combined with its beauty and flavor, make it a superlative culinary choice. The trade-off is that management is lagging in ensuring conservation.

In the Wild: Some consider mahimahi the world's most beautiful fish when it's alive, with its kaleidoscope of colors that flash and flush in electric yellows, blues, and blue greens. A fast, active, acrobatic fish, it travels near the surface in schools in offshore waters inhabited by billfishes, tunas, flying fish and the like. Mahimahi are found around the world in tropical and sub-tropical waters of the Atlantic, Pacific, and Indian oceans. Sometimes called dolphinfish, mahimahi is their Hawaiian name, which has come into widespread use to avoid confusion between the dolphin-the-fish and dolphin-the-mammal.

Mahimahi

Mahimahi live short, extreme lives. They grow fast, mature early, and, although no one really knows exactly, most believe they live only four years at most. And before those four years are up, they grow up to six feet long. They probably spawn year-round and are extremely fecund. A distinguishing feature between the sexes is the higher, squarer forehead in the males. For sustenance, they consume flying fishes, squid, crustaceans, and small fish. They congregate around floating logs, kelp mats, or anything floating at the surface. In the Atlantic, they particularly like to hang out underneath sargassum mats. Sargassum is a type of seaweed that frequently mats together in areas of the ocean where two water masses meet, and these micro-ecosystems frequently harbor a large diversity of living organisms seeking refuge and food.

fish names

Common Dolphinfish
(*Coryphaena hipparus*): mahimahi, dorado, dolphin (not to be confused with the mammals called dolphins)

 Mahimahi: fresh; frozen; boneless fillets; steaks

Macho Migrants

The U.S. seafood industry generates $100 billion at the consumer end, 67% of that through restaurants and 24% through retailers of fresh seafood (the rest through canned seafood, etc.).

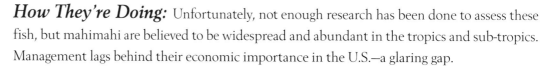

How They're Doing: Unfortunately, not enough research has been done to assess these fish, but mahimahi are believed to be widespread and abundant in the tropics and sub-tropics. Management lags behind their economic importance in the U.S.—a glaring gap.

How They're Caught: Mahimahi sometimes fall as by-kill in the tuna and swordfish longline fisheries in the Atlantic and Pacific. Now there's some directed longlining for the species. Fishers everywhere take advantage of the fish's known behavior of seeking floating structures and in Japan and elsewhere set out floating bamboo or cork platforms to attract them, making them easier to catch. Mahimahi have long been favorites of recreational rod and reel anglers. Recreational fishers take mahimahi by trolling, casting, or chumming from boats.

Although catches of mahimahi are tracked in records of catches for other pelagic species like billfish and tuna, as of this writing there was no management plan for these fish anywhere. As fishers increasingly target and catch mahimahi, the absence of any management could become problematic. That being said, it's worth noting that the South Atlantic Fishery Management Council has begun the long process of developing a plan to manage catches of mahimahi in U.S. waters off the East Coast. Pacific U.S. regulators have not made a similar effort, nor has any other country.

Special Issues: Longlines are being increasingly used to directly catch mahimahi and this will likely entail problematic by-kill of other species, as does most near-surface longlining.

Markets: Peru, Ecuador, Costa Rica, Japan, Taiwan, and the U.S. export mahimahi. U.S. domestic commercial catches come largely from Florida, Hawaii, and southern California. Other primary consumers are Japan, Europe, and the Caribbean region.

Can you really say "Fish is brain food"? YES.

Recent medical studies confirmed what American moms used to lecture. Fish—or more precisely, the Omega-3 fatty acids found in many fish—contribute to brain and nerve tissue development, especially in infants and children. One psychiatric study completed in 1999 found that Omega-3 fatty acids can act as mood stabilizers, providing short term relief from depression.

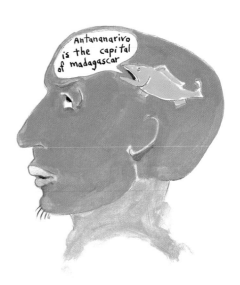

Shortfin Mako Shark

Sharks

OVERALL RECOMMENDATION:

All fall in the RED on the Audubon Fish Scale: don't bite these. They're long-lived, slow breeders, and many are over-fished and severely depleted.

In the Wild: Sharks are ancient creatures, having roamed our planet's waters since long before the age of dinosaurs. Today, 380 species are known to exist worldwide in all oceans and at all depths. Sharks live very measured lives: most are top-predators in their environments; they grow slowly; mature relatively late in life; and produce few offspring.

Sleek and torpedo-shaped, **shortfin makos** are cobalt blue, with silvery sides and white belly. They can grow over 12 feet long and reach a hefty 1,500 pounds, but most now weigh a mere 125 pounds or less—referred to as pups. They are found over continental shelves, canyons, and submarine peaks worldwide, where water temperatures range from temperate to warm—in the eastern Pacific from Washington to Chile, and in the western Atlantic. Makos mature around five years old and can live as long as 28 years. (Males mature when they're a little over six feet; females don't mature until they're nine feet long.) Embryos take up to a year and a half to develop inside the female, which gives birth to as few as four and as many as 16 pups every two to three years. By the time they emerge, they're already 26 inches long and ready to swim.

Thresher sharks are recognizable by the extremely long upper part of their tails—which is sometimes as long as the animal itself. Threshers use their sickle-like tail to herd and stun schooling fish upon which they prey. They grow to be 16 feet long (including their tail), and their pups are born alive already four feet long. Females produce only two to six pups at a time; how frequently is unknown. Scientists also don't know for sure how old threshers can

Mako, Thresher, and Blacktip Sharks: fresh or frozen; as steaks or fillets
Spiny Dogfish: fish and chips; fillets; and smoked in European markets
Fins of many shark species used in soup in Chinese restaurants

All Sharks →

*Thresher
Shark*

fish fact

Each year, sharks kill fewer than a dozen people worldwide. But people kill more than 100 million sharks. Most are killed for just their fins, primarily used as a thickener in expensive, high-prestige shark fin soup in Chinese markets.

get in the wild. These large sharks can be purple, gray, brown, bluish or black on top, with blue, gold or sliver sides and white undersides. Thresher sharks are found in the Pacific, Atlantic, and Indian oceans, and Mediterranean and Red seas.

The **spiny dogfish** is a small coastal shark found on both sides of the Atlantic as well as the Pacific and Mediterranean. Thought to be the world's most abundant living shark, it also has the longest gestation period of any animal: females stay pregnant for 24 months. These Atlantic sharks live as long as 35 years if they're male and 50 years if they're female, and do not mature until they're about 10 years old. Then, females give birth to an average of six live young. Interestingly, spiny dogfish in the Pacific can live 70 years.

Blacktip shark live from 10 to 18 years. Females mature at around seven years old. They stay pregnant for nearly a year after which they give birth to anywhere from two to seven pups. At the very most, a female blacktip shark will get pregnant six times over the course of her life. Off the U.S., blacktips frequent waters in the mid- and South Atlantic. They're the most common shark in the Gulf of Mexico and Caribbean waters.

How They're Doing. Sharks are vulnerable to intense fishing pressure: their populations quickly become depleted and require decades to recover. Many shark species, not just the ones highlighted here, are declining rapidly—and it's not just a domestic problem, it's an international one. Sharks are still being overfished nationally and globally despite clear evidence of their vulnerability to exploitation and the ecosystem effects their depletions can cause. Specifically, in the mid- to late 1990s, spiny dogfish in U.S. Atlantic waters declined dramatically and remain overfished, as do at least 22 of 39 shark species in the Atlantic. In the Pacific, the status of all shark species is unknown, but threshers, makos, and blue sharks off California show signs of overfishing.

*Small Spotted Catshark
(a common type of
European dogfish)*

HOW THEY'RE CAUGHT: A few kinds of sharks are caught for meat, and many are killed just for their fins for soup. Worldwide, commercial fishers directly target sharks mostly with longlines and drift gillnets. They're also frequently caught with longlines and drift gillnets targeting swordfish or tunas. Up until recently there was virtually no domestic management. The East Coast U.S. is officially but poorly managed relative to the sharks' needs, and for many species only their fins are kept and sold. Only four of the more than 125 fishing nations regulate shark fishing, and there is currently no management for shark fishing in international waters. International trade, especially in shark fins and dogfish meat, is driving U.S. shark fisheries.

West Coast commercial fishers take makos and threshers in drift gillnets and on longlines. There is no federal management of commercial shark fishing in the Pacific. State regulators recently instituted limits off California and Alaska. California instituted a ban on shark finning, wherein fishers catch sharks, cut their fins off and throw the sharks overboard to sink to the bottom and die. Fishers targeting sharks as well as tunas and swordfish, still legally "fin" in the central and western Pacific, around Hawaii, and in virtually all countries and international waters. Officials estimate that in 1998 alone, 60,000 of the 100,000 blue sharks caught in Hawaiian waters were finned and tossed back. And this keeps increasing each year. Hawaii is a critical center for the commercial flow of shark fins to Hong Kong.

Along the Atlantic Coast, the U.S. officiallly but poorly manages shark fishing. East Coast fishers catch dogfish with trawls and gillnets. Dogfish tend to school by size and sex, making the larger and more valuable adult females particularly vulnerable to overfishing. They used to be considered trash fish incidentally caught with New England groundfish and not kept, until strict controls of groundfishing forced fishers to turn their attention to dogfish whose catch was not managed. The already established European market for dogfish flesh for fish and chips transformed it practically overnight into an aggressive directed fishery. One could say dogfish are the Cinderella of the Northeast, starting out unwanted and ignored and rapidly becoming a popular target. Only in this case, dogfish are not living happily ever after. Larger females are preferred by European markets, and their removal jeopardizes the ability of the population to recover.

Makos and threshers are a favorite target of recreational fishers on private and party boats off the Atlantic and Pacific coasts. There's quite a culture around recreational shark fishing, wherein fishers take their boats offshore, and either troll slowly along or turn their motors off and drift with the winds and tide. To the boat cleat, the crew attaches big buckets with holes to allow the chum—frozen, ground-up fish—to bleed through slowly, creating a slick whose scent can attract sharks from miles around. At the end of hefty fishing lines are chunks of bluefish, mackerel, squid, or other fish with which to lure and catch the ultimate oceanic predator. It's now considered uncouth to bring in small immature sharks to the dock, as fishers are becoming more sensitive to the depleted state of these fantastic creatures. As macho a thing as it is to catch a shark, many recreational fishers fear their catch and use guns to shoot the hooked shark dead before bringing it to the boat. And, while there still are shark tournaments along the Atlantic and Pacific coasts, there are fewer nowadays—a reflection of the times and changing culture. Where many sharks caught in tournaments in years past would literally fill up garbage trucks, today most sharks are released alive and those that are brought to the docks are generally used for food for local charities.

fish fact

Dogfish comprises 95 percent of shark meat exported from the U.S.

fish names

Shortfin Mako
(*I. oxyrinchus*): Pacific mako, blue pointer, shortfin, bonito or mackerel shark

Thresher (*A. vulpinus*): sea fox, whiptail, or thintail shark

Spiny Dogfish
(*S. acanthias*): Cape shark, rock salmon, spurdog

Blacktip Shark
(*C. limbatus*)

Swordfish

Swordfish

In the Wild: Among the most spectacular and magnificent of the sea's creatures, swordfish (*Xiphias gladius*) can weigh in at 1,200 pounds and grow to lengths more than 15 feet. Their flat, pointed sword makes up a third of the fish's length. A dark, purple to bronze-like back lightens to gray on the sides and underneath. There is one species of swordfish worldwide. They are usually solitary, moving from the surface to 400 feet in depth, though they have been seen as deep as 2,000 feet. Swordfish live at least nine years, perhaps longer. They are thought to mature when they are about four feet long. In the Atlantic, sexual maturity is occurring at smaller and smaller sizes, a result of severe overfishing.

Several marlin species occur in tropical to temperate seas throughout the world. Striped, black, blue, white and hatchet marlin, spearfish and sailfish make up the rest of the billfish family. They are found in the Pacific from Peru to southern California, Hawaii to New Zealand and in the Indo Pacific. On the Atlantic side, billfish can be found from Cape Cod to the Ivory Coast of Africa and to Brazil and Venezuela.

How They're Doing: Swordfish are overfished and depleted in Atlantic. The status of swordfish and other billfish is unknown in most of the Pacific, but populations are believed to be fished at their full capacity. In 1997, a number of conservation groups launched a campaign to "Give Swordfish a Break," asking consumers and chefs not to buy or serve North Atlantic swordfish. The boycott was successful in helping to secure an international recovery plan for North Atlantic swordfish. They won't recover for ten years or more, and concerns remain that political pressure could reverse the advances only recently made.

Pacific
Swordfish

Atlantic
Swordfish

 Swordfish: fresh or frozen; steaks; loins; chunks; fillets and wheels; smoked

**OVERALL
RECOMMENDATION:**

RED in Atlantic because of depletion and bycatch problems. YELLOW in the Pacific due to bycatch.

**NUTRITION:
SWORDFISH**

130 calories
35 fat calories
total fat 4.5 g
40 mg cholesterol
22 g protein
Vitamin A 2%
Vitamin C 2%

(Based on a 3 oz. serving size. Vitamins and minerals are based on 2,000 calorie diet.)

Markets: Swordfish come into the U.S.—which is a primary consumer—from Chile, Japan, Brazil, Portugal, and Spain. Countries catching swordfish in the North Atlantic are the U.S., Spain, Canada, Portugal, and Japan. Brazil, Japan, Spain, Taiwan, and Uruguay dominate in the South Atlantic. Japan dominates the Pacific catches of swordfish, with China and Taiwan landing substantial numbers as well.

Special Issues: By-kill in swordfish fisheries is high. Most swordfish are caught with longlines and driftnets that catch large numbers of juveniles, sharks, turtles, and some mammals. Harpoon fisheries catch only older adults and entail no bycatch, but harpooning for swordfish is now almost nonexistent on both coasts due to declines caused by longlines and driftnets.

On Eating Them: Larger swordfish are prone to have high amounts of mercury in their flesh. The U.S. Food and Drug Administration set a standard for methyl mercury in food, and inspects imported swordfish. Anticipated future improvements in Atlantic management would move swordfish in the YELLOW in the near future.

Swordfish
(X. gladius)

Do swordfish and tuna contain mercury? YES.

All fish contain some amount of mercury and other elements found in nature. Mercury gets into the ocean, and subsequently into fish, from natural gasses released from the Earth's crust, and from burning wastes and fossil fuels. Fish get mercury in their tissues as water passes over their gills, and from what they eat. The larger the fish, the higher the level of methyl mercury. Because they are at the top of the food chain, swordfish, sharks and tunas tend to concentrate more of these elements. The U.S. Food and Drug Administration set the acceptable limit for methyl mercury in fish at one part per million (ppm). Swordfish that contain more than 1 ppm are not allowed to be imported into the U.S. (Domestically-caught fish are not subject to the same screening as imports.) Importers put a premium on fish smaller than 100 pounds because the smaller the fish, the lower the methyl mercury content. The top 10 fish species chosen by consumers all have levels of methyl mercury below 0.2 ppm. One would have to eat more than two pounds of them a week to reach harmful levels.

Some health professionals argue that studies setting safe mercury levels in fish are insufficient in that all the potential sources of human exposure to environmental and food pollutants were not taken into consideration. They say we don't know enough about how those interact over the long term to say what is safe. They've urged a phase-out of human activities that put additional metals and pollutants into the environment.

HOW THEY'RE CAUGHT

Managing swordfish catches in Atlantic waters of the U.S. is done via a federal plan for the entire coast, driven by international policy made by all the countries that fish for swordfish in the Atlantic. Managing swordfish catches and that of other billfish is essentially nonexistent in the Pacific, where much of the fishing takes place on the high seas by Japanese and Chinese longline vessels. Harpoons, handlines, and drift gillnets also are used to take swordfish. U.S. longliners catch swordfish off Hawaii and California, and coastal fisheries occur off Japan, Taiwan, Mexico, Chile, and Australia.

Bluefin Tuna

Tunas

Fish Scale

Troll-caught and Pole-caught Tuna

Other Tunas

In the Wild: Tunas, among the swiftest and strongest of animals in the sea, travel thousands of miles crossing the world's oceans. They are circumglobal, and occur in temperate to tropical waters of the Atlantic, Pacific, Southern and Indian oceans. Tunas are at the top of the oceanic food chain, and feed on mackerel, herring, and other fish. All five of the tuna species can be recognized by the rows of triangular "finlets" in front of their tails, giving them a spiky "robo fish" look.

The **albacore** sports a blue-black back with silver to gray sides and belly. Although sometimes weighing 100 pounds, the average market fish weighs ten to 30 pounds. Albacore are found in schools in temperate waters as far north as the Bay of Biscay in the Atlantic, along the west coast of the U.S. and off Hawaii. Unlike prolific tropical tunas, albacore live longer and grow slower.

Bigeye tuna, named for their oversized eyes, swim deeper than any of the other tunas. They, too, have blue-black backs, but flash a yellow pectoral fin. They're found in tropical and temperate waters off Chile, Ecuador, Peru, the Canary Islands, Hawaii, and New England. Less prolific or abundant than their cousins, bigeye frequent deep canyons and peaks 800 feet or deeper. The average market size is 100 pounds, but the record bigeye tipped in at 480 pounds.

Bluefin tuna are the giants of the tuna world, and perhaps of the entire fishy kingdom. These animals have been recorded at longer than 12 feet and weighing more than 2,000 pounds. The

OVERALL RECOMMENDATION:

In general, YELLOW on the Fish Scale because of inadequate management, high bycatch, and in some cases, severe depletion. But there are GREEN choices among the tunas if you're willing to carefully select from what's available. Best to stick with rod-and-reel-caught yellowfin, pole-caught skipjack, and trolled albacore. Much fresh and canned albacore is troll-caught, especially West Coast—but ask. Troll-caught and pole-caught are both easy GREENS.

Albacore, Skipjack and Yellowfin: canned; fresh or frozen steaks; sushi or sashimi
Canned "white tuna" is albacore; "chunk light" is yellowfin or skipjack.
Other tunas: fresh or frozen steaks; sushi or sashimi

so-called "average" bluefin weighs between 200 and 400 pounds. Known as southern bluefin in the Pacific, they swim in temperate waters off Japan, the Canary Islands, and in the Southern Ocean. On the Atlantic side, northern bluefin occur in the Mediterranean, off Newfoundland, Iceland, Norway, and the U.S. coast.

Skipjack make up half the catch of all tunas. Smaller and more barrel-shaped than other tunas, skipjack are deep purple to blue, with lavender blotches and dark stripes on their light undersides. They occur mostly in the southwest Pacific and around Hawaii, though they can be found in the southern Atlantic. Skipjack can reach 40 pounds, but most caught weigh a mere five pounds or so. They frequently school among other tunas.

Alabacore Tuna

HOW THEY'RE CAUGHT: Fishing for tuna happens year-round far out at sea with longlines, rod and reel, gillnets, or purse seines, depending on the region and the species. For example, most yellowfin destined for the can is taken with purse seines, while fish to be sold fresh or frozen is taken on longlines. Despite the importance of the tuna species as food fish and to national economies, and the long history of tuna fisheries around the world, management for these creatures is poor to non-existent.

Although there are several international management bodies that are supposed to conserve tunas, enforcement of even basic regulations like size limit is near to non-existent. Many of these management entities do little beyond scientific research. Except for eastern Pacific, basic data gathering is minimal. In most cases, the rules for tuna fishing are a matter of negotiation between countries with fleets catching the fish, and countries in whose waters they fish. Since tuna provide cash for developing countries, the conditions for allowing fishing are predictably relaxed. No management body has been successful in conserving abundance or rebuilding depleted tuna populations.

Recreational anglers avidly fish for tuna off the east and west coasts of the U.S. using similar techniques and gear as when they fish for sharks. Restrictions on sport fishing for tuna include size and catch limits.

fish fact

Some companies (e.g. Sainsbury's) sell canned skipjack labeled "pole caught."

Purse Seines: *Large nets that surround fish and are then drawn closed at the bottom like a purse, preventing fish from diving to escape.*

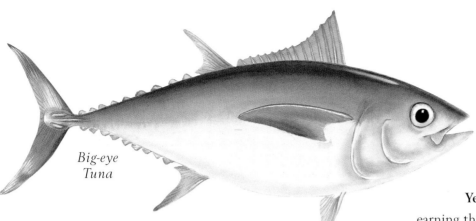

Big-eye
Tuna

Albacore *(T. alalunga):*
longfin tunny, and tombo

Big-eye *(T. obesus):* ahi

Bluefin *(T. thynnus):*
giant tuna

Skipjack *(E. pelamis):* aku

Yellowfin *(T. albacares):* ahi

Yellowfin are flashy members of the tuna tribe, earning their Hawaiian name "ahi," which means fire. Contrasting nicely against their blue backs, they sport a wide yellow stripe, yellow fins, and extra long versions of the two hindmost fins. Yellowfins are found in tropical waters off California, in the Gulf of Mexico, in the south Atlantic, off Hawaii and Ecuador, and in the western Pacific.

How They're Doing: Albacore are overfished in the Atlantic, and maxed out in the North and South Pacific. Bigeye tuna are overfished in both the Pacific and the Atlantic, and have declined substantially since 1950. Bluefin tuna are depleted in the Atlantic. Southern bluefin are depleted in the Southern Ocean and south Pacific, and designated as fully exploited in the west central Pacific. Skipjack tuna are abundant but declining in the Atlantic, abundant in the Pacific, and probably maxed out in the Indian Ocean. Yellowfin tuna are fully exploited in both the Pacific and Atlantic.

Special Issues: Yellowfin tuna congregate under schools of dolphin or around almost anything adrift, making it easier for fishermen to find them. These tunas are usually caught either by encircling pods of dolphins with nets or by encircling floating objects. Tuna caught by encircling dolphins (but not killing them) can now be legally sold in the U. S.

Bigeyes and Atlantic yellowfins are often taken on longlines, entailing generally high by-kill that includes fishes, sea turtles, and some mammals. Rod and reel-caught or "troll-caught" yellowfin and albacore entail low by-kill and are often sold fresh, and sometimes canned. All tuna longline fisheries have a high by-kill of sharks.

Markets: Tuna are caught and consumed worldwide. Almost all large bluefins, regardless of where caught, are sent to Japan for sushi. Single fish are often worth $10,000-$20,000 at dockside. One fishing boat received a record-breaking $80,000 for a single bluefin tuna.

Index